California Bar Examination

Essay Questions and Selected Answers

February 2015

The State Bar Of California
Committee of Bar Examiners/Office of Admissions

180 Howard Street • San Francisco, CA 94105-1639 • (415) 538-2300
845 S. Figueroa Street • Los Angeles, CA 90017-2515 • (213) 765-1500

ESSAY QUESTIONS AND SELECTED ANSWERS

FEBRUARY 2015

CALIFORNIA BAR EXAMINATION

This publication contains the six essay questions from the February 2015 California Bar Examination and two selected answers for each question.

The answers were assigned high grades and were written by applicants who passed the examination after one read. The answers were produced as submitted by the applicant, except that minor corrections in spelling and punctuation were made for ease in reading. They are reproduced here with the consent of the authors.

Question Number	Subject
1.	Contracts
2.	Real Property
3.	Civil Procedure
4.	Remedies
5.	Business Associations
6.	Wills/Trusts

ESSAY EXAMINATION INSTRUCTIONS

Your answer should demonstrate your ability to analyze the facts in the question, to tell the difference between material facts and immaterial facts, and to discern the points of law and fact upon which the case turns. Your answer should show that you know and understand the pertinent principles and theories of law, their qualifications and limitations, and their relationships to each other.

Your answer should evidence your ability to apply the law to the given facts and to reason in a logical, lawyer-like manner from the premises you adopt to a sound conclusion. Do not merely show that you remember legal principles. Instead, try to demonstrate your proficiency in using and applying them.

If your answer contains only a statement of your conclusions, you will receive little credit. State fully the reasons that support your conclusions, and discuss all points thoroughly.

Your answer should be complete, but you should not volunteer information or discuss legal doctrines that are not pertinent to the solution of the problem.

Unless a question expressly asks you to use California law, you should answer according to legal theories and principles of general application.

QUESTION 1

Marta operated a successful fishing shop. She needed a new bait cooler, which had to be in place by May 1 for the first day of fishing season.

On February 1, Marta entered into a valid written contract with Don to purchase a Bait Mate cooler for $5,500 to be delivered no later than April 15.

On February 15, Don called Marta and told her that he was having trouble procuring a Bait Mate cooler. Marta reminded Don that meeting the April 15 deadline was imperative. "I'll see what's possible," Don responded in a somewhat doubtful tone. Concerned that Don might be unable to perform under the contract, Marta immediately sent him the following fax: "I am worried that you will not deliver a Bait Mate cooler by April 15. Please provide your supplier's guarantee that the unit will be available by our contract deadline. I want to have plenty of time to set it up." Believing that Marta's worries were overblown and not wanting to reveal his supplier's identity, Don did not respond to her fax.

When Don attempted to deliver a Bait Mate cooler on April 16, Marta refused delivery. Marta had purchased a Bait Mate cooler from another seller on April 14, paying $7,500, which included a $2,000 premium for one-day delivery by April 15.

Have Marta and/or Don breached the contract? If so, what damages might be recovered, if any, by each of them? Discuss.

QUESTION 1: SELECTED ANSWER A

I. Governing Law

The UCC governs contracts for goods. The common law governs all other contracts, including contracts for services and real estate. The UCC has additional rules that apply when both parties are merchants.

Marta and Don entered into a contract to purchase a bait cooler. Because the bait cooler is a good, the UCC rules will govern this contract. Further, Marta is the owner of a successful fishing shop, and Don sells bait coolers. They can both be considered merchants and the UCC's merchant rules should also apply.

II. Contract Formation

A valid contract requires an offer, acceptance, and bargained for consideration. Under the UCC, goods that cost over $500 require that the contract be in writing to satisfy the Statute of Frauds.

The facts state that Marta and Don entered into a "valid written contract" to purchase the Bait Mate cooler. Marta and Don mutually assented for Marta to purchase a Bait Mate cooler for $5,500 to be delivered no later than April 15. Because the contract was for over $500 for a purchase of a good, the contract needed to be in writing to satisfy the Statute of Frauds, which Marta and Don satisfied.

III. Breach of Contract

A. Anticipatory Repudiation

A person who unequivocally states that they will not perform the contract before the time performance is required will have been considered to anticipatorily repudiate the contract. The other party who has not repudiated can treat this as a total breach and sue on the contract prior to the time of performance.

Two weeks after Marta and Don entered into their contract, Don called Marta and expressed his concerns in procuring a Bait Mate cooler. Marta told Don that meeting the April 15 deadline "was imperative" and Don merely responded that he would "see what's possible."

Marta may argue that Don anticipatorily repudiated the contract by telling Marta that he may not be able to perform on the contract before the contract was due. However, his statements were not unequivocal as to his inability to perform. Rather, Don only expressed doubt as to his ability to procure and deliver.

Because Don did not unequivocally state that he would not be able to deliver the Bait Mate cooler, he will not have been considered to have anticipatorily repudiated the contract.

B. Reasonable Assurances for Insecurity

Under the UCC, a buyer who has reasonable concerns or insecurity about the seller's ability to tender a good can request assurances that the seller will tender a good. The seller must offer the assurances within a reasonable period of time (generally no more than 30 days) or else the buyer who requested the assurances can treat the lack of assurances as a contract breach. The buyer has no duty to inform the seller that she is seeking to cover through the breach.

Here, Marta had reasonable concerns that Don would not be able to tender the Bait Mate cooler. Don himself raised his concerns about his possible inability to procure and deliver the good, and when Marta reminded him that she needed the cooler by April 15, Don did not assuage her concerns by stating that he would absolutely perform. Instead, he merely responded that he would see what was possible. Thus, Marta had reasonable concerns and was within her right to ask Don for further assurances.

Don, however, might point out that Marta demanded that he provide the supplier's guarantee that the unit would be made available by the delivery deadline. He did not want to reveal the identity of his cooler supplier and he believed that Marta's demand was unjustified. However, as discussed above, it was reasonable for Marta to have the concerns about Don's inability to deliver the contracted good. Accordingly, Don should have provided assurances and communicated his ability to tender the goods as contracted within a reasonable period of time. Don not only failed to respond to Marta in a reasonable time, he wholly failed to respond to her.

Don may counter that Marta should have informed him that she was treating his failure to respond as a breach of contract. However, Marta is not under any obligation to do so after not receiving assurances for her reasonable insecurity.

Because Marta had reasonable grounds to be insecure about Don's delivery of the bait cooler, Don should have replied to Marta within a reasonable period of time. Don failed to provide Marta any sort of assurance. Accordingly, Marta was justified in treating Don's lack of assurances as a breach.

However, if Marta did not have reasonable grounds to be insecure, and should not have treated the lack of assurances as a breach, then she can point out that Don breached the contract when he failed to deliver on April 15 (discussed below).

C. Failure to Tender the Good on the Contracted Date

The UCC requires that goods be perfectly tendered. This requires that the products have no defects and that they are delivered by the date required.

Marta can argue that even if she couldn't treat Don's failure to provide assurances as a breach, that Don breached the contract because he failed to deliver the cooler on the contracted date. Marta and Don's contract stated that Don would deliver *no later than April 15.* However, Don delivered on the 16th. By failing to tender delivery of the good by the contracted date, Marta can argue that Don breached and she isn't required to accept the good.

Don may argue that he substantially performed by delivering the day after, and in any case, the contract did not specify that time was of the essence. Further, he might argue that Marta was not harmed by the delay, because he still delivered the cooler before the first day of fishing season on May 1. However, Marta can correctly point out that those defenses such as substantial performance and delivery within a reasonable time frame after the contracted date where time is not of the essence is not applicable to UCC contracts. Perfect tender requires delivery on the contracted date. In any case, Marta may further counter that the contract was specific about the date the cooler needed to have been delivered. Additionally, she had made known through her fax communication in February that she needed the cooler on April 15 because she needed sufficient time to set up the cooler.

Because Don failed to perfectly tender the good, by not delivering the good on the contracted date, Don breached the contract.

D. Purchase of the Replacement Good Prior to Date of Delivery

Don might argue that it was Marta who breached the contract by purchasing a replacement cooler before the affected delivery date. However, as discussed above, if he failed to provide assurances for her reasonable insecurity, then Don was in breach and Marta was entitled to cover. If Don breached on April 15, Marta's cover purchase on the 14th should not be considered a breach of contract because Marta may still have been able to perform had Don delivered on April 15. However, Don did not deliver nor was Don aware of Marta's cover purchase.

IV. Damages for Contract Breach

A. Expectation

Where a contract has been breached, and the buyer is without the good and the seller has the good, the UCC provides that the buyer can receive expectation damages for the breach. This would place the non-breaching party in the position it would have been in had the contract been fulfilled. This can include the cost to cover and purchase the replacement good.

Here, Marta expended $7,500 to purchase a replacement Bait Mate cooler on April 14th. This included a $2,000 premium for the one-day delivery of the cooler by April 15. Marta paid $5,500 for the cooler itself, which is the same price she would have paid to Don for the same cooler. Marta then paid an additional $2,000 to have this cooler delivered within one day.

As to the cooler itself, Marta did not pay additional costs to actually cover for the replacement Bait Mate cooler. Thus, as to the cost of covering for the replacement cooler, Don would not be liable for any additional costs to cover the purchase of the replacement cooler.

Marta might argue that Don should be liable for the additional $2,000 it cost to deliver the Bait Mate cooler because this is the additional cost it required to have the cooler delivered by April 15, and place her in the position she would have been in had Don performed on the contract. Don will counter (as discussed below) that Marta did not mitigate her damages.

Consequential damages

A breaching party can also liable for the foreseeable indirect harm that results from the breach of contract. This might include, for example, economic harm that Marta's shop faced when she didn't have the Bait Mate cooler on the date contracted.

Here, it does not appear that Marta is alleging such losses that relate to Don's breach.

Incidental damages

A breaching party can also be liable for incidental damages, which cover the ordinary expenses the non-breaching party may have incurred in responding to the breach of contract. This includes the costs of inspection, the costs to return the non-conforming good, or the costs of negotiating with a new vendor to cover a good.

Marta does not appear to have additional incidental costs related to negotiating with the new supplier for the replacement cooler.

B. Duty to Mitigate Damages

The non-breaching party still has a duty to mitigate damages and minimize the costs that the breaching party will be liable for.

Here, Don might point out Marta breached her duty to mitigate the damages.

If Marta is correct in arguing that Don breached the contract by failing to provide assurances for her insecurity, Don will point out that the breach would have occurred when he failed to provide the assurances in a reasonable period of time. Marta demanded assurances in mid-February and Don never responded. Don will point out that if Marta is correct that he failed to provide necessary assurances, then he would have breached after that reasonable time period expired. We can assume that 30 days would be a reasonable response period. Accordingly, Don would have breached the contract in mid-March. However, Don can point out that Marta did not seek to replace the Bait Mate cooler until April 14.

Marta may argue that she had been looking for a replacement cooler and it wasn't until April 14 that she was able to enter into the contract. However, the facts do not indicate that Marta took those steps to replace the cooler. If Marta breached her duty to mitigate because she failed to try and cover earlier, then Don has a strong argument as to why he should not be liable for the $2000 premium Marta paid.

Further, Don might argue that if it wasn't reasonable that Marta demanded assurances, then his breach of contract did not occur until April 15, but Marta purchased the cooler on April 14. He might argue that he shouldn't be liable for Marta's premium purchase prior to the breaching date, but he could be liable had she purchased after the breach and paid a premium for the speedy delivery.

Don has a strong argument that Marta breached her duty to mitigate. Accordingly, Don may not be liable for the $2,000 premium Marta paid on her replacement cooler.

QUESTION 1: SELECTED ANSWER B

Governing Law

The UCC governs contracts for the sale of goods. Goods are tangible and moveable items. The common law governs all other contracts. If the UCC governs, certain rules will apply if the parties are merchants. Merchants are those who deal in the type of goods or have specialized knowledge or skill regarding the goods. Implied in every UCC contract is a covenant of good faith and fair dealing.

Here, there is a contract for a bait cooler. A bait cooler is a tangible good, and therefore, the UCC will govern this contract. Marta owns a fishing shop, which means she has specialized knowledge and skill and deals in the type of goods here (fish and fishing supplies), so she is a merchant. It is unclear is Don is a merchant. Marta has contracted with Don to purchase a bait cooler, but nothing in the facts indicate if Don is a commercial seller of bait coolers, or anything else to indicate his status as a merchant. However, because this is a very expensive cooler ($5,500), it is very likely that Don is a merchant seller of bait coolers. Also, because Don is procuring it for Marta, as opposed to having one personally and selling it online or by advertisement, that tends to show he is a merchant seller. Certain rules may apply relating to the parties as merchants. Also, because this is a UCC contract, there is an implied covenant of good faith and fair dealing.

Contract Formation

To have a valid contract, there must be mutual assent and consideration. Mutual assent is an offer and acceptance. An offer is a manifestation to presently have the intent to contract, with the terms clearly specified, communicated to the offeree. An acceptance is a manifestation to assent to the terms of the offer. Consideration is a bargained-for exchange, consisting of a legal value to one party and a legal detriment to the other. Consideration usually comes in the form of performance, forbearance, or a promise to perform or forbear.

Here, the facts indicate that a valid written contract was formed on February 1st; therefore, it can be inferred that there was a valid offer and acceptance. The consideration for the contract was the promise by Marta to pay the $5,500, and for Don to procure and sell to Marta a bait cooler.

Statute Of Frauds

Certain contracts must be in writing to be enforceable, signed by the party against who enforcement is sought. One such type of contract is a contract for the sale of goods over $500.

Here, the contract is for a good (cooler) for $5,500, which is over $500. The facts indicate that a valid written contract was entered into. Therefore, it is assumed that the statute of frauds is satisfied.

Anticipatory Repudiation

When one party gives a clear and unequivocal indication that he will not perform his end of the contract, the other party can treat that as an anticipatory repudiation, which is an instant breach of the contract. When this occurs, the non-breaching party may elect to not perform and immediately sue for damages, or to wait until performance is due and then sue for damages.

Here, On Feb 15, Don called Marta and told her that he was having trouble procuring the cooler. Marta reminded Don that there was a strict deadline of April 15, and Tom told her he would "see what is possible", using a doubtful tone. Because these words are not a clear and unequivocal indication that Don would not perform, there is not an anticipatory repudiation. To have an anticipatory repudiation, Don would have had to say something more along the lines of "I will not be able to procure the cooler by April 15". Because Don's words did not amount to an anticipatory repudiation, Marta cannot treat the contract as breached as of Feb 15. However, she can demand assurances.

Reasonable Grounds For Insecurity and Demand for Assurances

When a party has reason to believe the other party may not be able to perform, typically actions by the other party that fall short of an anticipatory repudiation, the party may, in writing, demand assurances of performance by the other party. If commercially reasonable, the demanding party may suspend performance. Additionally, if the party who has given reasonable grounds for insecurity does not provide assurances within 30 days, the other party may treat that as an anticipatory repudiation and immediately treat the contract as breached, even if the time for performance has not come.

Here, Don's words to Marta on the phone did not amount to an anticipatory repudiation (above), but, they certainly gave Marta reasonable grounds for insecurity. At the time the contract was formed, Marta and Don agreed that the cooler would be delivered no later than April 15. On the Feb 15 phone call, Marta again reminded Tom of the strict deadline. When Tom, using a doubtful tone, said he will see what is possible, this gave Marta reasonable grounds for insecurity. Marta was worried that he would miss the deadline and she would not have time to set the cooler up and ready for the first day of the fishing season. Marta faxed Don, which meets the writing requirement, asking him to provide assurances of performance by providing his supplier's guarantee that the unit will be available. Don believed that this was overblown and did not respond. Marta will argue that Don needed to provide assurances within 30 days. Because Don did not respond, Marta can treat the contract as repudiated as of 30 days after the fax, which would be March 15. Don did not want to give up his supplier's identity, and may argue that although Marta's grounds for insecurity are reasonable, that her demanding his suppliers guarantee was unreasonable. Don is assumingly in the business of procuring items for fishing shops, and he will argue that if he gave up his suppliers identity, Martha may go straight to the supplier in the future for her needs and circumvent Don. A court could go either way on deciding this issue. A court will surely find that Marta had reasonable grounds for insecurity, but may find that her demand for assurances (providing the supplier) was not reasonable. However, the court would likely find that Don doing nothing, and not responding at all, was also reasonable and not in good faith.

If Don did not want to give up his supplier, he still could have replied and given Marta assurance that he would perform by the deadline.

It is most likely that a court would find that Don failing to respond to Marta's insecurity within 30 days amounted to an anticipatory repudiation. In that case, Marta could treat the contract as breached immediately and find other options for her cooler, and sue Don for damages. However, even if the court finds that it did not amount to a repudiation, Don will still be in breach of the contract for delivering late.

UCC Perfect Tender

In UCC contracts, there must be a perfect tender of goods; otherwise there is a breach. A perfect tender means every item is delivered as promised, and at the correct time. When there is not a perfect tender, the non-breaching party may take the non-conforming goods and sue for damages, reject some goods and keep some, or reject all the goods and sue for damages. The non-breaching party must notify the seller of the breach and if they are going to accept or reject the goods, and if they reject, must timely return the goods, arrange for the goods to be shipped back, hold the goods for pickup, or re-sell on the breaching party's account.

Here, Don attempted to deliver the cooler on April 16th, one day late of the strict deadline. Because Don did not deliver on the agreed deadline (April 15), he did not make a perfect tender. Therefore, Don has breached, and Marta is under no obligation to accept the cooler. The facts indicate that Marta promptly notified Don that she was refusing delivery, as required by the rules.

Damages

Marta's Damages Claims

When a UCC contract has been breached, the non-breaching party may sue for and receive compensatory damages. The most common compensatory damages are expectation damages, incidental damages, and consequential damages.

Expectation Damages

Expectation Damages put the non-breaching party in the position they would be had the contract not been breached. Expectation damages must be foreseeable, certain, and mitigated. When the seller has breached, the expectation damages would normally be the fair market value of the good minus the contract price, or the cost to cover minus the contract price.

Here, Don and Marta contracted for the sale of the cooler for $5,500. Because Don did not perform by the deadline of April 15, and because he likely repudiated when he did not respond to Marta's request for assurances, Marta was entitled to either sue for the difference in the fair market value of the cooler and the contract price, or to cover and sue for the difference between the cost of cover and the contract price. Here, Marta covered and purchased a different cooler for $7,500. Marta will argue that Don is liable to her for the difference of $2,000. Don may argue that he should not be liable for this difference, because the fair market value (and the price it appears Marta paid) of the cooler was actually only $5,500; the $2000 extra was a one day rush delivery fee. Marta will argue, however, that she had no choice but to pay the $2,000 delivery fee, since she needed it by April 15th. Don may also argue that if the court does find he repudiated as of March 15th, that Marta did not mitigate, because she could have found another cooler between March 15 and April 15th, but instead, she waited until April 14th to purchase the cooler with 1 day rush. Marta may respond that when there is a repudiation, she has the option to wait until performance is due to treat the contract as breached. However, Don will then argue that because she bought the new cooler on April 14, not April 15th, that she was not waiting for performance. Also, Don will likely successfully argue that Marta MUST have been relying on the anticipatory repudiation, and not on the perfect tender breach, since she did not wait until his performance was due on the 15th to purchase the new cooler.

A court could go either way. Don may have to pay Marta the $2000 difference for what she paid and the contract price, but, the court also might find that Marta did not mitigate, and therefore the $2000 rush fee was avoidable. However, if Marta did in fact look around for coolers between March 15 and April 15 and just could not find one until April 14, then she will have met her duty to mitigate and could recover the $2,000.

Incidental Damages

Incidental damages are those damages that are incidental to the breach, and are always expected, such as costs to return or store the goods.

If Marta incurred any incidental costs, such as advertising that she was looking for a cooler, or long distance calls to other suppliers, etc., then she will be able to recover these costs also.

Consequential Damages

Consequential damages are special damages that are unique to the non-breaching party, such as lost profits, and they must be foreseeable at the time of contracting to the breaching party to be recoverable.

It does not appear that Marta suffered any consequential damages as a result of the breach, but if she did, and they were foreseeable, then she could recover these too.

Punitive Damages

Punitive damages in contract cases are not recoverable. Marta will not be able to recover any punitive damages, because they are not available in breach of contract actions.

Don's Damages Claims - Restitution

Restitution is an equitable remedy meant to prevent unjust enrichment. Typically, this type of remedy is used when a contract is unenforceable, and one party received a benefit but did not have to pay for it. In such a circumstance, the other party can usually receive the reasonable value of their services. At common law, the breaching party could not receive restitution. But, modernly, many courts will provide reasonable value of services even to the breaching party to prevent unjust enrichment by the non-breaching party.

Here, Don may argue that he is entitled to something from Marta, since he procured the cooler, and likely had to pay for the cooler from his supplier to get it for Marta. However, Marta will successfully argue that she was not unjustly enriched in any way, because she did not get anything from Don. She did not keep the cooler. Don may then try to argue that the services he provided in spending the last few months procuring the cooler were valuable services, and that he should be compensated for the procurement services. However, a court will likely find this a very weak argument, as Don breached the contract, and Marta received absolutely no benefit from Don.

QUESTION 2

Amy and Bob owned Blackacre in fee simple as joint tenants with a right of survivorship. Blackacre is located in a jurisdiction with a race-notice recording statute.

Without Bob's knowledge, Amy gifted her interest in Blackacre to Cathy by deed. Amy and Bob then sold all of their interest in Blackacre by a quitclaim deed to David, who recorded the deed. Shortly thereafter, Cathy recorded her deed.

David entered into a valid 15-year lease of Blackacre with Ellen. The lease included a promise by Ellen, on behalf of herself, her assigns, and successors in interest, to (1) obtain hazard insurance that would cover any damage to the property and (2) use any payments for damage to the property only to repair such damage. Ellen recorded the lease.

Five years later, Ellen transferred all of her remaining interest in Blackacre to Fred. Neither Ellen nor Fred ever obtained hazard insurance covering Blackacre. While Fred was in possession of Blackacre, a building on the property was destroyed by fire due to a lightning strike.

David has sued Ellen and Fred for damages for breach of the covenant regarding hazard insurance for Blackacre.

1. What right, title, or interest in Blackacre, if any, is held by Cathy, David, Ellen and/or Fred? Discuss.

2. Is David likely to prevail in his suit against Ellen and Fred? Discuss.

QUESTION 2: SELECTED ANSWER A

1. What right, title, or interest in Blackacre, if any, is held by Cathy, David, Ellen and/or Fred?

At common law, there were no recording statutes and the rule was that the first in time prevailed. Under this jurisdiction, there is a race-notice statute that will govern the facts of this case. If the statute does not apply, then the common law does. A race-notice statute provides that any subsequent purchaser of property will take if they are a bona fide purchaser (BFP) and recorded first. To be a BFP, a party must pay value and take without notice of any prior recordings that may affect their title to the property. Notice can be by: (1) actual notice; (2) constructive notice; or (3) inquiry notice. Actual notice is that the party knew there was another party with a claim on the property. Constructive notice is when a recording in the grantor-grantee index gives notice to a party that there are other parties claiming interest to the land. Lastly, inquiry notice is when the party is given facts that there may be other possessors to the property and that party has a duty to inquire further (i.e., if they see a house built on the land with occupants, that party has a duty to inquire why they are on the land).

A. Cathy

A joint tenancy is created with a right of survivorship when the four unities are met: time, title, instrument and possession. In other words, the parties must acquire their joint tenancy at the same time, with the same amount of title, in the same instrument and each have the right to possess the entire land. The right of survivorship allows that when one of the joint tenants die, the entire estate goes to the surviving joint party. However, if the joint tenancy is severed, the parties become tenants in common and the right of survivorship no longer exists. The joint tenancy can be severed by a unilateral conveyance of one of the joint tenants to another party.

Here, Amy and Bob owned the land in fee simple as joint tenants with the right of survivorship. The facts do not give details as to if the four unities of time, title, instrument and possession were met. However, the facts assume that these elements were met. As such, Amy and Bob owned Blackacre as joint tenants with the right of survivorship to begin with. Amy thereafter gifted her interest to Cathy. This bequest severed the joint tenancy between Amy and Bob. At this point in time, Bob and Cathy were then owners to Blackacre as tenants in common. However, as will be discussed in the following section, because Cathy failed to record her deed, David will take Blackacre under the recording statute and Cathy has no interest in Blackacre.

B. David

As mentioned, under the recording statute in this jurisdiction, a subsequent purchaser will take if they are a BFP and record their interest first. Amy and Bob sold all of Blackacre to David. Although Amy no longer had any interest in Blackacre because she had conveyed her interest to Cathy, David was unaware of that fact. David was a BFP as required under the statute. First, he paid value for the property. And secondly, based on the facts, he did not have knowledge about Cathy's conveyance. There are no facts to indicate that he had actual knowledge of the conveyance to Cathy. Additionally, David did not have constructive notice of the conveyance to Cathy. A BFP only has a duty to check the grantor-grantee index when the conveyance is made to him. He does not have to subsequently check the index for good title. Therefore, when he checked the index before accepting the property, there was no notice of Cathy's deed. Lastly, David did not have inquiry notice. It doesn't appear that Cathy lived on the land or made any assertions of title over the land. As such, David qualified as BFP because he took without notice and paid value for the land. Also, to prevail under a race-notice statute, the subsequent purchaser must record. Here, David recorded his deed promptly. As a result, David's interest in the land is superior to Cathy's.

C. Ellen

David had good title to the property as discussed above and therefore, was free to do what he wanted with the land. He subsequently leased the property to Ellen. Ellen is a BFP under the recording statutes as well. She is paying value for the lease through rent payments and took without notice of Cathy's interest. Similar to David, there is no actual or inquiry notice for the same reasons as stated above. Additionally, she just not have constructive notice. Although Cathy has now recorded the deed, it is not within the chain of title that Ellen would have to search. Even if Ellen did have notice of Cathy's interest, she would be protected by the Shelter Doctrine, which allows subsequent parties to assume BFP status from the prior conveyance, even if that purchaser did not have BFP status. Here, David was a BFP and recorded his deed; thus, Ellen is a BFP under David anyway.

However, David's conveyance to Ellen was not a fee simple, but rather, a lease for a term of 15 years. Thus, by the terms of the lease, Ellen has a possessory interest in the property for the next 15 years. At the time of the lease, she was in privity of contract with David (through the lease) and privity of estate with David (by occupying the land).

D. Fred

Parties are generally free to assign their interests under a contract or lease to another party. An assignment is where a party gives the remaining interest under the lease to a subsequent party. Alternatively, a sublease is where a party gives less than the full interest left on the lease. Thus, the courts are to look at the actual interest conveyed and not what the parties might have labeled it.

The lease between David and Ellen did not contain an anti-assignment clause. Rather, the lease applied to Ellen, her assigns, and successors in land. Thus, an assignment of Ellen's interest was valid under the lease. (Even if it wasn't, David would have likely waived the anti-assignment provision because he continued to accept rent from Fred). Additionally, the facts state that Ellen transferred "all her remaining interest in Blackacre to Fred." Therefore, it was an assignment, since all her interest, the remaining 10 years on the lease, was transferred to Fred. As such, Fred assumed Ellen's interest in the land. As such, Fred is lawful tenant with possessory interest in Blackacre for the next ten years.

E. Conclusion

Because this is a race-notice jurisdiction and the statute applies under the facts of this case, David has superior title to the land. Cathy does not have any interest in the land because she failed to record her interest. David conveyed his possessory interest to Ellen, who assigned her interest to Fred. As such, David holds title in fee simple to Blackacre and Fred has possessory interest in Blackacre for the next ten years under the terms of the lease between David and Ellen.

2. David v. Ellen & Fred

As mentioned above, there was a valid assignment of Ellen's interest to Fred under the lease. Ellen, as the assignor, remains in privity of contract with David. Fred, as the assignee, remains in privity of estate with David. The terms of the lease between David and Ellen contained two covenants: Ellen, on behalf of herself, assigns, and successors was to: (1) obtain hazard insurance that would cover any damage to the property and (2) use any payments for damage to the property only to repair such damage. Neither Ellen nor Fred ever obtained hazard insurance covering Blackacre. Unfortunately, lightning struck the property and destroyed a building on the property. Thus, the issue is whether David can prevail on a damages claim based on these covenants against Ellen and Fred?

A. Ellen

As mentioned, Ellen remains in privity of contract with David under the terms of the lease. A novation occurs when two parties agree that one party will no longer be held liable under the terms of the contract.

Under the facts, Ellen and David entered into a 15-year lease agreement. Five years into the lease, Ellen assigned her interest to Fred. There does not appear to be any agreement between David and Fred relieving Ellen of her liability under the lease. As such, no novation has occurred. Because David and Ellen are still in privity of contract, David can bring claims against Ellen for damages for breach of the covenant regarding hazard insurance for Blackacre.

B. Fred

For a covenant to run with the land and bind successors in interests, certain requirements must be met depending on whether the interest in the burdened (servient) or benefited (dominant) estate is being transferred. The servient estate is the estate that incurs the burden of the covenant, while the dominant estate is the one that benefits from the covenant. If the covenant is on the servient estate, the covenant will run with the land if: (1) the parties intended the covenant to run with the land; (2) the covenant touches and concerns the land; (3) the servient estate has notice of the covenant; (4) there exists horizontal privity; and (5) vertical privity.

Here, the covenant burdens the lessee estate, since Ellen and her successors/assigns are required to maintain hazard insurance and use that insurance to repair the damages. Thus, David will have to show the above five elements in order to be able to collect damages from Fred.

i. Intent

The parties to the original agreement must have intended that the covenant be perpetual and continue to bind successors in interest of the land. Here, the parties specifically included in the written lease agreement that "Ellen, on behalf of herself, assigns, and successors in interest" will maintain hazard insurance and use the proceeds of such insurance to fix any damage caused by any hazards. Therefore, the express language of the parties in the lease provide that they intended the covenant to bind all successors in interest.

ii. Touch and Concern the Land

To bind successors in interest, the covenants must also touch and concern the land. Courts have held that a covenant touches and concerns the land if it conveys a benefit onto the land. For example, the payment of rent is a sufficient covenant that touches and concerns the land. Here, the covenant is to provide insurance to protect the land in case of damage and to repair the land in the event that such hazardous damage does occur. This is for the benefit of the land to maintain the premises and therefore, it touches and concerns the land.

iii. Notice

The successor in interest must have notice of the covenant in order to be bound by the terms of it. As mentioned above, there are three types of notice. Here, Fred had constructive notice because Ellen recorded the deed in the grantor-grantee index.

Therefore, Fred would be able to know the terms of the lease because it was within the chain of title and will be deemed to have constructive notice of the covenants.

iv. Horizontal Privity

Horizontal privity must exist between the original parties to the covenant, such as grantor-grantee or lessor-lessee. A covenant agreement alone is insufficient to establish horizontal privity. Here, David and Ellen have horizontal privity as their relationship was that of lessor-lessee. Thus, horizontal privity exists.

v. Vertical Privity

Lastly, vertical privity must exist between the successor in interest and the previous owner of the servient estate. Here, Ellen conveyed the remainder of her interest on the lease to Fred. Therefore, there is a vertical privity between Ellen and Fred.

Thus, all five elements are met for a covenant to run with the land and David may hold Fred liable for damages for the breach of the covenants.

C. Conclusion

David may hold Ellen liable for damages for breach of the two covenants because she is in privity of estate with David. Additionally, David will be able to hold Fred liable for damages because the two covenants run with the land and Fred had notice of such covenants.

1. **What right, title, or interest in Blackacre, if any, is held by Cathy, David, Ellen and Fred.**

Classify the Interest: Joint Tenants with a Right of Survivorship

A joint tenancy is a concurrent interest in land in which case at least two individuals own an undivided interest in the whole of the property. A joint tenancy is created with express language that the tenancy carry with it the right of survivorship. The right of survivorship means that when one joint tenant dies the other co-tenants take the deceased tenant's interest in the property. A joint tenancy is created when four unities are present at the time of creation. These unities are the unities of time, title, interest, and possession.

Here, facts indicate that Amy and Bob owned Blackacre in fee simple as joint tenants with a right of survivorship. Thus, the original property relationship was that of a joint tenancy because the right of survivorship was expressly provided for.

Severance of the Joint Tenancy

A joint tenancy is severed whenever any one of the four unities of time, title, interest, and possession is disturbed. When one of the four unities of a joint tenancy is disturbed a tenancy in common results and the right of survivorship is extinguished. In this event the tenants in common own a undivided interest in the whole of the property which is then freely alienable.

Here, the facts indicate that Amy gifted her interest in Blackacre to Cathy by deed. By gifting her interest in the joint tenancy, Amy disturbed the four unities, particularly the unity of title. As indicated above, when a joint tenancy is severed a tenancy in common is created. Thus, since the joint tenancy was severed, at this particular point in the facts

Amy held no interest, and Cathy and Bob held the property as tenants in common. The right of survivorship was extinguished and both Cathy and Bob had an undivided interest in the whole of the property.

Amy's Conveyance to David / Recording the Interest / Recording Statute

The facts indicate that after Amy gifted her interest in Blackacre to Cathy by deed she and Bob sold all of their interest in Blackacre to David. These facts implicate the rules for the relevant recording statue.

In a race-notice jurisdiction, a subsequent bona fide purchaser (BFP) is protected by the recording statute provided that he takes without notice and is the first to record his interest in the deed. There are three different kinds of notice. There is actual notice, record notice, and inquiry notice. Actual notice refers to the extent to which a BFP actually knows that someone else claims an interest in the land. Record notice refers to the extent to which the BFP is notified by researching the record of title. And inquiry notice refers to the extent to which a BFP inspects the property and discovers someone else asserting a claim to the property. Additionally, it should be noted that the recording statutes are designed to protect subsequent BFP's and not gratuitous grantees of real property.

Here, the facts indicate that Amy and Bob sold all of their interest in Blackacre to David after Amy gifted her interest to Cathy by deed. The facts also indicate that David recorded his deed before Cathy recorded her deed. Thus, for the recording statute to apply and for David to take title to the property he must be a subsequent BFP who took without notice and who recorded first. The facts indicate that David did in fact record before Cathy recorded. Thus, the "recorded first" element is satisfied. The next question that must be determined is whether David had notice of Amy's interest. There is nothing in the facts which says that David had actual notice of Cathy's interest. Additionally, although the facts do not indicate that David inspected the property, the facts also do not indicate that Cathy occupied the property so as to put David on notice had he inspected the property. The real question is whether David had record notice. Determining record notice is a two-step process. First, the BFP must go to county recorder's office, locate the particular property and construct the chain of title. The chain of title can be constructed by looking first at the grantee index and then building the chain of title back in time. Next, the BFP must adverse each link of the chain. This is done by looking at the Grantor index and following the chain of title until the BFP reaches his interest. Here, David will not discover Cathy's interest in Blackacre. Cathy recorded her deed too late. By recording her deed after David recorded his deed David would not be put on notice as to Cathy's interest in Blackacre. Also, although not directly relevant, it should be noted that Cathy, as a gratuitous grantee, is not likely to receive any protection under the recording statute.

On balance, David obtained lawful title to Blackacre as a subsequent BFP who took without notice and was the first to record his interest.

2. Is David Likely to Prevail in his Suit Against Ellen and Fred

The Lease with Ellen

A tenancy for years is a specific type of tenancy that has a specific start date and a specific end date. A tenancy for years need not be for a terms of actual years but rather only needs a specific starting and ending date. A tenancy for years is terminated upon the end of the specified date.

Here, the facts indicate that David entered into a valid 15-year lease of Blackacre with Ellen. Since the lease has a specific start date, and a specific end date, it is likely considered a tenancy for years.

Ellen's Transfer to Fred

A sublease is a legal relationship in a leased property that arises when the tenant conveys out less than his entire interest under the lease. In this circumstance, sublessor has privity of estate with the lessor. An assignment occurs when the lessor conveys out all of his durational interest under the lease. In the case of an assignment the original lessee is no longer in privity of estate with the lessor but depending on the circumstances may still remain in privity of contract with the lessor. Privity of estate means that two individuals share an interest through their relationship to a leased property and privity of contract is a contract obligation between two contracting parties.

Here, the facts indicate that five years into the lease, Ellen transferred all of her remaining interest in Blackacre to Fred. Thus, because all of the remaining interest was transferred as opposed to only some or part of the interest Ellen executed a valid assignment. The results of this assignment is Fred is not in privity of estate with David. However, because Ellen was the original contracting party with David, she remains in privity of contract with David.

Breach of the Covenant: Ellen

A restrictive covenant is a written promise with respect to land either to take an affirmative action or to refrain from taking action. Liability for the restrictive covenant may attach to parties that are either in privity of contract with the lessor or privity of estate. In the event of privity of contract, the contracting party remains liable under a contract theory of recovery. If an express contract between the lessor and the lessee is breached by failing to satisfy the written covenant then the landlord may sue to evict the tenant and/ or assert a claim of money damages.

Here, as noted above, Ellen is in privity of contract with David. She is the original party under the lease, who signed the lease and who had knowledge of the covenants in the lease. The fact that she assigned her interest to Fred means only that she is not under privity of estate with David, but she is still liable under privity of contract. The lease included a promise by Ellen to obtain hazard insurance and to use any payments for damage to the property to repair such damage. Ellen breached the lease covenant because she never obtained hazard insurance covering Blackacre and because a building on the property was destroyed by fire.

Thus, because Ellen is in privity of contract with David, David can elect to sue Ellen for breach of the express contractual covenant.

Breach of the Covenant: Fred

Restrictive Covenant

A restrictive covenant is a written promise with respect to a particular piece of property to do or to refrain from doing something on that particular property. Restrictive covenants run with the land to successive assignees if the covenant makes the land more beneficial or useful. In order for the burden of a restrictive covenant to apply there must be intent and notice, the covenant must touch and concern the land, there must be vertical privity and horizontal privity. In order for the benefit of a restrictive covenant to apply there need only be the elements of intent, touch and concern and vertical privity. Vertical privity is present when the successor in interest has the entire interest in the property. Horizontal privity refers to the fact that the original parties to the agreement had a mutual interest in the property outside of the covenant agreement.

Here, the facts indicate that the lease expressly stated that the covenant to obtain hazard insurance and to use its proceeds would apply to "Ellen, on behalf of herself, her assigns, and successors' interest." Thus, because there was intent that the covenant apply to subsequent parties, the intent element is met. The facts also indicate that Ellen recorded the lease and that the covenants were expressly written in the lease. Thus, it appears that Fred had notice of the lease provisions. The next element that must be satisfied is the touch and concern element. As discussed above, in order for the covenant to touch and concern the property it must make it more beneficial or more useful. Here, the covenant was that Ellen and her assigns obtain hazard insurance which would cover any damage to the property. If a particular piece of property is covered by insurance, then it is more likely than not to be benefitted and thus, as a result will be more valuable. As noted above, vertical privity must also be satisfied. Here, Ellen conveyed out all of her remaining interest on Blackacre. Additionally, there is nothing in the facts to suggest that anyone else other than Fred not presently occupies the property. Thus, vertical privity is satisfied. Finally, there must be horizontal privity. David owns the property outright. Additionally, David and Ellen had no interest in the property outside of the lease. Thus, horizontal privity is satisfied.

Based on the foregoing analysis, it appears that the burden of the restrictive covenant to obtain hazard insurance does run to Fred, a party in privity of estate with David. Thus, because Fred failed to obtain insurance and because the property was destroyed implicating the need for the insurance, David is likely to prevail in his suit against Fred.

QUESTION 3

In March, while driving her car, Diana struck and injured Phil.

In April, Phil filed a complaint against Diana in federal district court properly alleging diversity jurisdiction and seeking damages for negligence for physical injury.

In May, Diana filed an answer denying negligence.

In June, during discovery, Diana filed a motion asking the court to order (1) a physical examination and (2) a mental examination of Phil. Over Phil's objection, the court ordered him to submit to both examinations.

In July, Diana served Phil with a notice to depose Laura, a physician who treated him after the accident. Phil objected on the grounds that (1) Laura could not be deposed because she was not a party, and that (2) deposing her would violate the physician-patient privilege. The court overruled Phil's objections.

In September, a few weeks before trial, Phil decided to file a demand for a jury trial. Diana immediately filed a motion to strike the demand. The court granted Diana's motion.

1. Did the court err in granting Diana's motion to order (a) the physical examination and (b) the mental examination of Phil? Discuss.

2. Did the court err in permitting Diana to depose Laura? Discuss.

3. Did the court err in granting Diana's motion to strike Phil's demand for a jury trial? Discuss.

QUESTION 3: SELECTED ANSWER A

Applicable law

Under the Erie doctrine, a federal court sitting in diversity jurisdiction must apply the substantive laws of the state where it sits and the procedural laws of the federal system, generally the Federal Rules of Civil Procedure and in most cases the Federal Rules of Evidence. Whether or not a rule is substantive or procedural is a balancing test that depends on whether 1) the rule is outcome determinative, 2) the federal court's interest in applying their own rules, and 3) whether or not application of the federal rule will result in forum shopping.

Whether or not a party may obtain an order for a physical or mental examination is a rule of discovery that is procedural and governed by the Federal Rules of Civil Procedure which will apply in this case.

a) Diana's motion for a physical examination of Phil

Under the Federal Rules of Civil Procedure, a party may obtain a mental or physical examination of the other party if 1) that party's physical or mental condition is in controversy, and 2) good cause exists for ordering the examination. Good cause will generally be found to exist if the examination in question is not overly intrusive and it is relevant, measured in terms of its logical and legal relevance as well as how relevance is defined under the Federal Rules of Civil Procedure with regard to its discoverability. Evidence is logically relevant if it tends to make the existence of a fact of consequence more or less likely. Evidence is legally relevant if its probative value is not substantially outweighed by its prejudicial effect. And evidence is relevant and discoverable if it is reasonably likely to lead to the discovery of admissible evidence.

Phil's suit against Diana is one for personal injury stemming from her alleged negligence. In a negligence suit, the plaintiff must prove duty, breach, cause, and damages. Because damages are a required element, the injury and the extent of the injury suffered by a party will always be in controversy in a personal injury suit. Additionally, good cause exists for ordering the physical examination here. It is not overly intrusive as Phil has already likely sought out and received medical treatment for his injuries of a similar nature in this case. Additionally, it is logically and legally relevant and relevant under the Rules' definition for discovery because it is reasonably likely to lead to the discovery of admissible evidence. The examining physician may have a different opinion as to the nature and extent of injuries suffered by Phil.

For these reasons, the court did not err in granting Diana's request for a physical examination of Phil.

b) Diana's motion for a mental examination of Phil

With regard to Diana's motion for a mental examination of Phil, the rules are the same as for a physical examination. Under the Federal Rules of Civil Procedure, a party may obtain a mental or physical examination of the other party if 1) that party's physical or mental condition is in controversy, and 2) good cause exists for ordering the examination. However, the calculus here for a mental examination is much different.

Phil's suit against Diana is for personal injury. His physical condition is relevant because it is a fact in controversy as damages are an element of negligence. Phil's mental condition, however, does not appear to be in controversy. Phil's suit is not for infliction of emotional distress or any other cause of action where his mental condition would be a fact in controversy. If Phil suffered from some sort of mental disease or defect that made him comparatively or contributorily negligent or that affected his abilities to perceive or recall, such that Diana could impeach his credibility, then Phil's mental condition could theoretically be in issue. However, that does not appear to be the case here. There is nothing to indicate that Phil's mental condition is in controversy. Additionally, a mental examination is an intrusive procedure that should not be granted unless necessary to establish a claim or defense, neither which requirement is met in this case. Good cause for granting Diana's request for a mental examination thus cannot be said to exist.

For these reasons, the court erred in granting Diana's request for a mental examination of Phil.

2)

Whether the physician-patient privilege applies

Under the Federal Rules of Evidence, there is no physician-patient privilege. There are only privileges for spousal communications, spousal immunity in criminal cases, penitent-clergy, and patient-social worker.

However, as discussed above, under the Erie doctrine, a federal court sitting in diversity jurisdiction must apply the substantive laws of the state where it sits and the procedural laws of the federal system. Generally the Federal Rules of Civil Procedure and in most cases the Federal Rules of Evidence are procedural. However, whether or not a testimonial privilege applies is a rule of substantive law and a federal court sitting in diversity must apply the law of the state in which it sits regarding testimonial privileges.

The federal court sitting in this case must apply the state law regarding the doctor-patient privilege. Generally the doctor-patient privilege covers confidential communications between a doctor and a patient for the purposes of obtaining medical treatment. If the state in which this federal court sits acknowledged the doctor-patient privilege then Phil's communications to his doctor would generally be privileged.

However, there is generally an exception to the privilege when the patient-plaintiff's physical condition is in controversy. As stated above, this is a personal injury suit and damages are a necessary element of the negligence claim so Phil's physical condition is in actual controversy.

For that reason, even if the doctor-patient privilege applies, Phil's communications to Laura would likely be outside the privilege and would not prevent Diana from deposing Laura.

<u>Whether Laura cannot be deposed because she is not a party</u>

As with the standard for granting a physical or mental examination of a party, whether a party can be deposed is a discovery rule and is thus procedural and governed by the Federal Rules of Civil Procedure.

The Federal Rules of Civil Procedure allow a party up to 10 depositions in a case. Each deposition must be no longer than 1 day of 7 hours. A party may depose another party at any time simply by providing reasonable notice. A party may depose a non-party, but it must be done on subpoena to the non-party and must provide reasonable notice and accommodations.

Under the Federal Rules of Evidence, Laura may be deposed even though she is not a party to the litigation. So Phil's objection is not correct.

However, there is no indication in the fact pattern that Diana obtained a subpoena or served it on Laura prior to deposing her. Diana cannot simply serve Phil with a notice of subpoena in order to depose a non-party.

Nonetheless, a party's objection to discovery must be stated accurately and with particularity. Phil may have waived his valid procedural objection to Diana's deposition of Laura by not correctly stating the grounds for his objection.

In sum, Diana may depose Laura under the Federal Rules of Civil Procedure, even though she is a non-party. However, Diana must do so on subpoena and notice to Laura, which Diana failed to do in this case. However, Phil incorrectly stated the basis for his objection to Diana deposing Laura and in so doing likely waived his otherwise valid procedural objection to the deposition.

Thus, the court did not err in permitting Diana to depose Laura.

3)

Under the 7th Amendment to the Constitution, a party is entitled to a jury trial in all suits for damages at law. Phil's suit against Diana is a personal injury suit for damages at law and not for some form of equitable relief like an injunction so Phil is entitled to a jury trial in his suit against Diana (as is Diana). However, under the Federal Rules of Civil Procedure, a party must file a demand for a jury trial within 14 days of the filing of the answer to the complaint. A party may file a motion to strike all or a portion of the other party's pleading within 30 days of receiving that party's pleading.

In this case, Diana filed an answer to Phil's complaint denying negligence back in May. Phil did not file his demand for a jury trial until September and only a few weeks before trial. For this reason, Phil's demand is untimely and absent good cause for the delay in this case, which does not seem likely, Phil has waived his right to demand a jury trial. Since Diana immediately filed her motion to strike in response to Phil's demand, it was timely and should be considered and granted by the court.

For this reason, the court did not err in granting Diana's motion to strike Phil's demand for a jury trial.

QUESTION 3: SELECTED ANSWER B

Preliminary matters

Applicable Law

After having been injured by Diana (D), Phil (P), filed a complaint in April against D in federal district court properly alleging diversity jurisdiction and seeking damages for negligence for physical injury. As such, because the complaint was filed in federal court, the Federal Rule of Civil Procedure (FRCP) govern the rules applicable to the proceedings and the actions of the courts and the parties in the suit.

(1) The Court Properly Granted Diana's Motion to Order (a) the physical Examination if she properly established good cause, but erred in granting (b) the mental examination

(a) The Physical Examination

Scope of Discovery

Discovery is the process by which parties obtain information from the other party. The FRCP provides for a broad scope of discovery, and the information needs only to be relevant to the cause of action. In fact, any information that would reasonably lead to the discovery of admissible evidence is discoverable. In other words, the information does not have to be admissible evidence to be produced, but only to reasonably lead t such information. Here, the dispute between P and D involves a car accident where D struck and injured P. As a result, P filed an action against D for negligence for physical injuries. Therefore, any information that would relate to the accident, the physical condition of P, which is at issue here, will be admissible. Here, D has filed a motion, seeking a court order directing the court to order a physical examination of P. Such examination is relevant because here, the physical condition of P is at issue since the lawsuit involves damages for personal injury. As such, this information is discoverable and within the scope of discovery.

Physical Examination Requirements

Physical Condition at Issue

In order for a party to obtain an order for a physical examination, the FRCP requires, first, that the physical condition be at issue. Here, P's condition is at issue because, as explained above, the lawsuit between P and D is about a car accident where D stuck and injured P. P is seeking damages. A physical examination will be useful to determine the extent of the injury cause by the accident to P, and will therefore be useful to determine the extent of damages, if any. Also, such physical examination will also determine if the physical injuries suffered by P were the result of the accident.

Court order and Showing of Good Cause

The FRCP requires that a court grant a motion to order a physical examination only when the moving party establish good cause to do so. Here, the facts are not clear on whether D established such good cause. A showing of good cause will require D to show that there is no other means to obtain the information that the physical examination would provide and establish the reasons to do so. Here, as explained above, a physical examination will be useful to determine the extent of the injury caused by the accident to P, and will therefore be useful to determine the extent of damages, if any, especially if there is no other information available. Also, such physical examination will also determine if the physical injuries suffered by P were the result of the accident. However, if the deposition of D is ordered (see below), then the showing of good cause for a physical examination will harder to establish because there would already be available information related to the physical condition of P after the accident. If ordering the deposition fails, however, this might constitute a good cause to order the examination because no information related to P's physical condition would therefore be available.

(b) The Mental Examination

Scope of Discovery

Discovery is the process by which parties obtain information from the other party. The FRCP provides for a broad scope of discovery, and the information needs only to be relevant to the cause of action. In fact, any information that would reasonably lead to the discovery of admissible evidence is discoverable. In other words, the information does not have to be admissible evidence to be produced, but only to reasonably lead t such information. Here, the dispute between P and D involves a car accident where D struck and injured P. As a result, P filed an action against D for negligence for physical injuries. Therefore, any information that would relate to the accident, the physical condition of P, which is at issue here, will be admissible. Here, a request for a mental examination is not likely to lead to any relevant admissible information. In fact, here, the mental condition of P is not at issue, only his physical condition because he is seeking damages for personal injury as a result of the accident. As such, this demand does not fall within the scope of discovery.

Mental Examination Requirements

Again, a court will issue an order for mental examination, only when this condition is at issue and when the moving party has established good cause to do so. Here, as explained above, the mental condition of P is not at issue and there is no reason why the court would order such examination. Not only does it fails to show good cause but would also be highly prejudicial to P.

(2) The Court Erred in Permitting to Depose Diana only if a Subpoena was not Issued, and P's argument that the Deposition would lead to the discovery of Privileged information fails

Scope of Discovery

Discovery is the process by which parties obtain information from the other party. The FRCP provides for a broad scope of discovery, and the information needs only to be relevant to the cause of action. In fact, any information that would reasonably lead to the discovery of admissible evidence is discoverable. In other words, the information does not have to be admissible evidence to be produced, but only to reasonably lead t such information. Here, the dispute between P and D involves a car accident where D struck and injured P. As a result, P filed an action against D for negligence for physical injuries. Therefore, any information that would relate to the accident, the physical condition of P, which is at issue here, will be admissible. Here Diana (D) is a physician who treated P right after the accident. Her deposition will be useful because it will lead and explain what was the physical condition of P right after the accident and will help in determining the extent of the injury as well as damages, if any.

Deposition of Third Party - Subpoena To The Third Party

The FRCP allows deposition of non-party to the case and provides for a maximum of 10 depositions, no longer than 7 hours each. There can also be only one deposition per person. When the deposition involves a non-party, i.e. someone not named in the lawsuit, then the requesting party must request the court to issue a subpoena in order to depose the third party. Here, D served P with a notice to depose Laura (L), the physician who treated him after the accident. The FRCP allows "notice" only when the discovery tools are used by party against another party. When a third party is involved, a subpoena is required, which D shall have done to properly depose her. In fact, not only did she fail to notice Laura personally, but she also failed by the means she used. As such, P is wrong when he says that a third party cannot be deposed. A third party can be deposed but here the court erred in granting the discovery request because the third party, Laura, was not properly notified.

Limit of The Scope of Discovery = Privileged Communication

The broad scope of discovery is limited by privileged information. In fact the FRCP provides that discovery means: discovery of any "non privileged" information. As such, whenever a privileged communication is involved, the scope of discovery may be limited. Here, P is asserting the Physician-Patient Privilege. As explained in the preliminary considerations, the FRCP apply here. The FRCP, and the Federal Rules of Evidence, do not recognize a Physician-Patient Privilege. As such, whether this argument will fail or prevail depends on which law the Federal District Court will apply.

Diversity Cases - Erie Doctrine - Application of State Law Privilege

The lawsuit filed by P against D was filed in federal district court, and properly alleged diversity jurisdiction. Under the Erie Doctrine, Courts sitting in diversity jurisdiction will apply the federal procedural law, and the substantive law of the state. Whether a law is substantive or procedural depends on whether it is outcome determinative or not. State Law regarding privileges have been held to be outcome determinative and therefore, substantive law for purposes of Erie Doctrine. Here, assuming that the state law of the seat of the federal action recognizes the physician-patient privilege, the federal court will have to apply it and such privilege might limit the scope of discovery.

Physician-Patient Privilege

Privilege

The physician-patient privilege is a privilege usually applied by states specifically recognizing such privilege. Under the physician-patient privilege any communication between a physician and his patient, made for the purpose of diagnosis or treatment, is privileged. The patient is the holder of the privilege and can oppose to the revelation of such information. Here, deposing L will likely lead to revealing privileged information: P saw L for purposes of diagnosis and treatment after the car accident and therefore, such communications are likely privileged.

Exceptions

The Physician-Patient privilege does not apply in several circumstances, and especially when the physical condition of the patient is at issue. Here, as explained, P's physical condition of D is at issue: the lawsuit involves a car accident where D struck and injured P and P is seeking damages for physical injury. As such, the privilege does not apply and P will fail in his argument that the deposition of L will lead to violate the physician-patient privilege because here, the privilege does not apply.

(3) The Court Properly granted Diana's Motion to Strike Phil's demand for a jury trial

In September, a few weeks before trial, P decided to file a demand for jury trial. D immediately filed a motion to strike the demand. The court was absolutely right in granting the motion.

7th Amendment Right to a Jury Trial

The 7th Amendment of the U.S. Constitution provides a right for a jury trial in federal civil case (does not apply to the states through the 14th Amendment) when the damages at law involved exceed $20. Here, P is seeking damages for personal injury under a negligence action. Negligence is an action recognized in common law and the damages required are legal damages and likely to involve more than $20, since they stem from the personal injury suffered after the car accident. Therefore P was entitled to a jury trial, but only as long as the demand was timely filed.

Notice to Opposing Party and Timely Demand

P made his demand for a jury trial about 3 weeks before trial. A demand for jury trial must be noticed to other party and promptly filed. The FRCP requires that a demand for a jury trial be filed by the Plaintiff 14 days after the complaint is filed, at the very latest and be properly notified to the opposing party. Here, P made his demand only 3 weeks before trial, after all the pleadings were closed. As such, this was not a timely demand and the Court was absolutely right to grant D's motion to strike P's demand for a jury trial.

QUESTION 4

Steve owned two adjoining improved tracts of land, Parcels 1 and 2, near a lake. Parcel 1 bordered the lake; Parcel 2 bordered Parcel 1, and was adjacent to an access road. Steve decided to sell Parcel 1 to Belle. Belle admired five 100-year-old oak trees on Parcel 1 as well as its lakefront location.

On February 1, Steve and Belle executed a contract for the sale of Parcel 1 at a price of $400,000. The contract specified that the conveyance included the five 100-year-old oak trees. In addition, the contract stated that Belle was to have an easement across Parcel 2 so that she could come and go on the access road. Although the access road was named Lake Drive, Steve and Belle mistakenly believed that it was named Top Road, which happened to be the name of another road nearby. The contract referred to the access easement as extending across Parcel 2 to Top Road, which would not have been of any use to Belle. The contract specified a conveyance date of April 1.

Later in February, Steve was approached by Tim, who offered Steve $550,000 for Parcel 1. Steve decided to breach his contract with Belle and agreed to convey Parcel 1 to Tim. Despite Belle's insistence that Steve honor his contract, he told her that he was going ahead with the conveyance to Tim in mid-April, and added, "Besides, our contract is no good because the wrong road was named."

In March, Belle learned that, in April, Steve was going to cut down the five 100-year-old oak trees on Parcel 1 to better the view of the lake from Parcel 2.

1. What equitable remedies can Belle reasonably seek to obtain Parcel 1? Discuss.

2. What legal remedies can Belle reasonably seek if she cannot obtain Parcel 1? Discuss.

QUESTION 4: SELECTED ANSWER A

1. What equitable remedies can Belle reasonably seek to obtain Parcel 1? Discuss.

Equitable Remedies

Remedies are ordinarily split into two categories, equitable remedies and remedies at law. Equitable remedies are only available where a remedy at law is inadequate to repair the harm. Equitable remedies are decided by the judge whereas legal remedies are usually decided by a jury. Unlike legal remedies that usually only declare damages owed from the defendant to the plaintiff, equitable remedies are backed by the contempt power of the court. If a defendant fails to comply with an equitable order, she can be held personally in contempt of court. There are several equitable remedies that Belle may seek to protect her rights with respect to the land sale contract for Parcel 1 with Steve.

Temporary Restraining Order (TRO)

A temporary restraining order is a stop gap measure wherein a court can order a defendant not to act, or occasionally to act affirmatively, in order to preserve the status quo until a hearing on a preliminary restraining order can be heard. A temporary restraining order will only be granted where the plaintiff can demonstrate that (1) she will suffer irreparable harm without the order, (2) the balance of the equities between the plaintiff and defendant favors the order, (3) the plaintiff is likely to prevail on the merits of her claim. A temporary restraining order can be heard ex parte if the plaintiff demonstrates a good faith attempt to give notice or demonstrates good cause for not giving notice. A temporary restraining order is a time-limited measure, typically limited to ten days. In this case, Belle might seek a TRO to stop Steve from cutting down the trees on Parcel 1 and not to sell Parcel 1 to Tim or any other buyer.

Irreparable Harm

First, Belle must demonstrate irreparable harm. In other words, she must show that a remedy at law would be inadequate and, without this order, any further remedy would be inadequate. Belle can demonstrate irreparable harm with respect to the cutting down of trees because her contract specifically protects her right to the 100-year-old oak trees and the trees were important to her decision to purchase the property. If Steve cuts down the trees, they cannot be replaced by damages. It would take another 100 years to grow similar oak trees. Belle likely also can show irreparable harm regarding Steve's selling of the property. Belle seeks to enforce her contract to purchase the property. If Steve sells the property to another bona fide purchaser in the meantime, she will not be able to seek specific performance. Steve may argue that he is not planning to sell to Tim until mid-April; therefore a TRO is not necessary. However, Belle can reasonably argue that Steve is not acting in good faith and there is a possibility that he will expedite the sale in order to deprive Belle of her right to specific performance. Therefore, Belle can demonstrate irreparable harm.

Balance of the Equities

Next, Belle must demonstrate that the balance of equities tips in her favor. In other words, Belle must prove that the hardship on her of not receiving the TRO is greater than the hardship to Steve of the TRO. Belle will argue that if the trees are cut down or the property is sold, she will forever lose the benefit of her contractual bargain. Therefore, there is a strong equitable argument in favor of granting Belle the TRO. Steve will argue that a TRO is inequitable because he will lose the right to an improved view of the lake on his property and might lose his interested buyer. However, a TRO will only interrupt Steve's view for a short time if he is able to prevail later and Steve is unlikely to lose his buyer based on this short time-limited order and if he does, there are likely other buyers available. The court may also disfavor Steve's arguments because he is breaching his contract with Belle and therefore his equitable arguments are not as strong. As such, the balance of the equities tips in favor of Belle.

Likelihood of Success on the Merits

Belle must demonstrate that she is likely to succeed on the merits. Belle will be able to prove a likelihood of success on the merits. A valid contract requires offer, acceptance, and consideration and must not be subject to any valid defenses. The land sale contract signed by both parties demonstrates offer and acceptance and satisfies the Statute of Frauds. The contract provides for the exchange of $400,000 for a parcel of land, which satisfies the bargained-for exchange requirement. The contract requires Steve to transfer the land to Belle and specifically protects Belle's rights to the five oak trees. Nonetheless, Steve has unequivocally plans to cut down the trees and sell to another buyer. As such, he has anticipatorily breached. If Steve receives notice, he may argue that the contract is not valid because of the mistake in the contract with respect to the name of the road. Such a mutual mistake, however, does not invalidate the contract. Therefore, Belle can establish a likelihood of success on the merits.

Preliminary Injunction

A preliminary injunction is a longer lasting pre-judgement equitable remedy. A preliminary injunction is a court order restraining the defendant from action (or more rarely, requiring the defendant to affirmatively act) to preserve the status quo. It lasts until there is a final judgment on the merits. The requirements for a preliminary injunction are identical to those for a temporary restraining order: (1) irreparable harm, (2) balance of the equities and (3) likelihood of success on the merits. However, a preliminary injunction requires notice to the defendant and a hearing.

As discussed above, Belle can demonstrate irreparable harm, balance of the equities, and likelihood of success on the merits. To receive a preliminary injunction, Belle will have to give Steve notice and the court must hold a hearing. Steve will argue that the contract is invalid because of the mistake regarding the name of the road for the easement and therefore, Belle is unlikely to succeed on the merits. But Belle can seek reformation of the contract to correct that error. Even if she could not prevail on reformation, the mistake is only harmful to Belle; therefore Steve cannot void the contract on the basis of this mistake, only Belle can. Therefore, Steve's argument will not be successful. Belle will likely be successful in receiving a preliminary injunction pending the court's determination of Belle and Steve's right to Parcel 1.

Contract Reformation

Contract reformation is an equitable remedy wherein the court will correct an error in a written contract in order to conform the contract with the actual agreement of the parties. Reformation is most often available where there is an error in the contract on the basis of a mutual mistake or scrivener's error. A mutual mistake occurs where both parties intend the contract to reflect an agreement between them but, due to a mistake by both parties, the contract does not properly reflect this agreement.

Belle can argue that the land sale contract should be reformed to include an easement over Parcel 2 to reach Lake Drive rather than Top Road. She can demonstrate to the court that both she and Steve intended the contract to include an easement over Parcel 2 to reach the access road adjacent to Parcel 2, which is Lake Drive. Both Steve and Belle mistakenly thought that the adjacent access road was called Top Road. Therefore, she can demonstrate the proper elements of mutual mistake to justify the reformation.

Steve will argue that the parol evidence rule bars extrinsic evidence related to the contract where there is a written contract. This argument will not be successful because the parol evidence rule does not apply in cases related to contract reformation. Belle can successfully seek reformation of the contract.

Specific Performance

Next, Belle will seek specific performance of the contract. Specific performance requires the defendant to actually perform under the contract rather than pay legal damages for the breach. Specific performance is available where there is (1) a valid contract, (2) that is sufficiently definite in its terms, (3) all conditions have been met for defendant's performance, (4) that there is no adequate remedy at law, (5) enforcement is feasible and (6) it is not subject to any equitable defenses.

As discussed above, Belle has a valid contract for the sale of the land for $400,000. There are no valid defenses as Steve's theory on the basis of mutual mistake fails because Belle can reform the contract and he cannot invalidate the contract on the basis of a mutual mistake that only injures Belle. The contract is sufficiently definite. The contract clearly describes the parcel of land to be sold (with the oak trees intact), the parties, and the price and payment information. Finally, Belle must be prepared to pay the purchase price to satisfy the condition of Steve's performance.

Belle has no adequate remedy at law. Every piece of land is unique. Therefore, land sale contracts are per se unique and damages are per se inadequate for a buyer (and seller under the theory of mutuality of remedies). As such, Belle can easily establish inadequate remedy at law. The enforcement of specific performance here is certainly feasible because it only requires a single transaction. Courts are hesitant to grant specific performance for repeated transactions and will never allow specific performance for personal services. But these concerns are not present; enforcement is feasible.

Finally, there must be no equitable defenses, specifically the defenses of laches and unclean hands. The defense of laches bars specific performance or other equitable remedies where the plaintiff has unjustifiably delayed in bringing the action and the delay prejudices the defendant. There is no indication that Belle has delayed since she will bring this action before the closing of the contract was even due. There is no prejudice to Steve. The defense of unclean hands bars specific performance where the plaintiff is guilty of some wrongdoing, even if not technically a breach or illegal act, in relation to the transaction. In this case, there is no suggestion of any wrongdoing by Belle. The only mistake she made with respect to the contract was entirely unintentional and innocent. This defense does not apply. Belle can seek specific performance of the contract.

If Steve cuts down the trees, Steve may argue that he is excused from specific performance of the contract because it would be impossible for him to perform the contract. However, where complete performance is not possible, a plaintiff seeking specific performance can still seek specific performance of the contract to the extent possible and seek abatement of the purchase price based on the damages from incomplete performance. Therefore, even if Steve cuts down the trees, if Belle still wants the property, she can seek specific performance and request that the court value the trees and abate the price accordingly. Of course, Belle will have to establish the value of the trees with reasonable certainty, which may be difficult given the intangible aesthetic benefit of the trees.

2.   What legal remedies can Belle reasonably seek if she cannot obtain Parcel 1?

Expectation Damages

If Belle does not obtain Parcel 1, she can seek legal remedies instead. A land buyer's legal remedy for the seller's breach of contract is ordinarily expectation damages. Expectation damages seek to put a non-breaching party in the same position they would be in but for the breach. In land sale contracts they are calculated by the difference in the fair market value of the land and the contract price for the land. In this case, Belle needs to establish the fair market value of the land. A reasonable estimate for that might be the recent offer from Tim for $550,000. Therefore the difference would be $150,000 ($550,000-$400,000). Belle is entitled to the return of any deposit and $150,000 in damages, that will put her in the same legal position as if the contract was performed.

Belle may also seek consequential damages that arise from the breach if they were reasonably foreseeable. Since it is unclear what Belle bought the property for, it is unclear whether or not she could prove any consequential damages. If she was purchasing for a business purposes, she may seek to prove lost profits from the delay in finding a new property. Any lost profits claim would be limited by a defense of foreseeability and reasonable certainty.

Reliance or Restitution Damages

Where a buyer is unable to prove expectation damages, perhaps because the market price is below the contract price, a buyer can seek reliance damages for the breach. Reliance damages seek to put the buyer in the same place she was before the contract was made. Most often in land sale contracts, the reliance damages are the out-of-pocket expenses including any down payment or earnest money paid to the seller. Where a seller breaches in good faith, for example because he is unable to deliver marketable title due to no fault of his own, a buyer may also be limited to her reliance damages. In this case, expectation damages are appropriate because Belle can prove that the fair market value is greater than the contract price and Steve's breach was not in good faith.

Finally, restitution damages are available where other remedies are inappropriate and inadequate and the defendant has been unjustly enriched by this action. In this case, restitution damages would include the return of her down payment. If Steve actually sells to Tim, they may also include the additional $150,000 in profits that Steve gained from breaching his contract with Belle and selling to Tim.

The most typical defenses available to damages in contract cases are failure to mitigate damages or uncertainty. In this case, neither will apply. There is no evidence that Belle failed to act in any way that ran up her damages and by seeking the difference in fair market value and the contract price, the damages are reasonably foreseeable.

QUESTION 4: SELECTED ANSWER B

1. Equitable Remedies

The issue here is what equitable remedies Belle may seek to obtain Parcel 1.

Temporary Restraining Order

A temporary restraining order ("TRO") is an order from the court requiring, or forbidding, the nonmoving party to take an action, while the nonmoving party seeks a preliminary injunction. The purpose is to preserve the status quo pending a decision on the motion for a preliminary injunction. To obtain a TRO, a plaintiff must show (1) that, without the TRO, she will suffer imminent irreparable harm, as balanced against the hardship that the defendant will suffer from the issuance of the TRO, and (2) a likelihood of success on the merits. A plaintiff may seek a TRO *ex parte* - that is, without notice to the nonmoving party - if, in addition to showing a likelihood of irreparable harm, the plaintiff shows a strong showing for why notice could not be practically provided, or why it should not have to be provided (for example, if issuing notice would cause the defendant to take the action causing irreparable harm). A TRO is only available for up to 10 days (or 14 days, under the Federal Rules of Civil Procedure).

Irreparable Harm

Here, Belle purchased the property from Steve in part because they contained the five 100-year-old oak trees. If Steve cut them down, it would prevent Belle from enjoying their presence on the property. Because they are so old, they could not be readily replaced; instead, should she have to plant new ones, she would need to wait 100 years to have comparable trees on the property. Thus, she would suffer irreparable harm should Steve cut them down.

Moreover, Belle would suffer irreparable harm if Steve sold the property to Tim. If Tim did not know about the prior contract (that is, if he was a bona fide purchaser for value), and Steve sold him the property, the sale would be valid, and Belle would not be able to recover the property. Even though the conveyance to Tim will not occur until mid-April - and thus, is not scheduled to occur until after the 10-day TRO would dissolve - Belle would successfully argue that the TRO is still necessary to prohibit Steve from accelerating the sale in light of the pending litigation.

In contrast, there is no similar risk of harm to Steve. Regardless of the outcome of the litigation, Steve is either going to sell the property to Belle or to Tim in April. Preventing him from cutting down the trees will only obstruct his view of the lake for a period of less than two months, which is a minor inconvenience at most. Moreover, he will not suffer irreparable harm if he cannot convey the property immediately to Steve.

Thus, Belle would show the irreparable harm required for a TRO.

Likelihood of Success on the Merits

Belle would also be able to show a likelihood of success on the merits. Steve and Belle appear to have a valid contract, and Steve has breached the contract. Moreover, Steve's defenses here are limited.

First, under the Statute of Frauds, contracts for the conveyance of land must be in writing and signed by the party against whom enforcement is sought. The facts suggest that the contract was in writing, but they do not say so expressly. To the extent that the contract was not in writing or signed, Steve might raise the Statute of Frauds as a defense. But, because the facts suggest a writing, this is unlikely to be successful.

Second, Steve might argue that the contract is void because of the parties' mutual mistake. A contract is void for mutual mistake if both parties were mistaken to a material fact and the party seeking to invalidate the contract did not bear the risk of mistake. Here, even though the parties made a mistake in the writing, they both subjectively understood which road was meant to be included in the contract; and, in any event, as the property owner with superior knowledge, Steve likely bore the risk of mistake. Thus, Steve's defense would likely fail. Belle would likely succeed on the merits.

Conclusion

Belle can seek a TRO to stop Tim from cutting down the trees and conveying the property to Tim.

Preliminary Injunction

A Preliminary Injunction ("PI") is an order from the court requiring, or forbidding, the nonmoving party to take an action, in order to preserve the status quo pending trial on the merits. The test for a PI is similar to that for a TRO. A plaintiff must show (1) that, without the PI, she will suffer imminent irreparable harm, as balanced against the hardship that the defendant will suffer from the issuance of the PI, and (2) a likelihood of success on the merits. Unlike a TRO, however, a PI may not be issued ex parte.

For the same reasons described above, the court would grant Belle a PI pending trial.

Specific Performance

Specific performance is an equitable remedy that requires the breaching party to perform his or her obligations under the contract. To obtain specific performance, a plaintiff must show (1) that there was a valid contract with sufficiently certain terms, (2) that the plaintiff performed or was able to perform her obligations under the contract, (3) no adequate remedy at law, and (4) feasibility of enforcement. Also, specific performance is not available if the defendant has any equitable defenses.

Valid Contract

To be sufficiently definite, a land sale contract must identify the parcel to be conveyed, the purchase price, and the parties. Here, the contract specified all three. Moreover, as described above, the contract appears to be valid and Steve does not appear to have any defenses to formation. Thus, the first prong is met.

Performance

Even though Belle has not yet paid the purchase price, there is nothing in the facts to suggest that she is not able or willing to fulfill her obligations and pay the contract price. Thus, the second prong is met.

Inadequate Remedy at Law

Under the law, all land is considered unique. Moreover, here, the parcel had unique features - it was near a lake and had 100-year-old oak trees. It would be impossible for Belle to obtain another identical parcel. Thus, simply awarding her monetary damages would not be an adequate remedy. She has no adequate remedy at law.

Feasibility of Enforcement

Requiring specific performance here would be feasible. It is not clear whether the parcel is in the same state as the court but, in any event, the court has personal jurisdiction over Steve and can require him to convey the property to Belle. Thus, enforcement is feasible.

Defenses

In some cases, a court will not award specific performance if it will result in undue hardship to the defendant, resulting from the plaintiff's sharp practices. Here, Steve might argue that he would suffer undue hardship if he cannot obtain the value of his separate bargain. But he has not shown any sharp practices by Belle, and simply forgoing another opportunity is not a sufficient hardship to constitute a defense to specific performance. Thus, Steve does not have any defenses to specific performance.

Conclusion

Belle can obtain specific performance and require Steve to sell her the property.

Reformation

Reformation is an equitable remedy where the court will reform the terms of the agreement to reflect the true understanding of the parties. It requires (1) a showing of the mutually-understood contractual terms and (2) valid grounds, such as a mistake in rendering the contract to writing. Parol evidence may be used to show the existence of such a mistake.

Here, even though the contract identified the easement as giving Belle access to "Top Road," this was plainly not the true understanding of the parties. The parties both believed that the contract was giving Belle an easement to access the road known as "Lake Drive." Thus, there was a true meeting of the minds here and a court would be able to use parol evidence to determine that this was the true intent of the parties. Thus, the court would reform the contract to substitute "Lake Drive" for "Top Road."

2. Legal Remedies

The issue here is what is the appropriate measure of damages, should Belle not be able to obtain equitable relief.

The standard measure of contract damages is the expectancy measure. The purpose of contract damages is to put the non-breaching party into the same position she would have been in had the contract been fully performed. In a land sale contract, the expectation measure is the difference between the contract price and the fair market value of the property at the time of sale.

Here, Tim offered to purchase the property for $550,000. The fact that a buyer was willing to pay this price is strong evidence that it is the fair market value. Accordingly, should Belle not be able to obtain specific performance, she would be able to obtain monetary damages from Tim totaling $150,000 - the difference between the contract price and the fair market value. She would also be able to obtain any incidental damages resulting from the breach (for example, the transaction costs of cancelling the sale).

QUESTION 5

Andy, Ruth, and Molly decided to launch a business called The Batting Average (TBA), which would publish a monthly newsletter with stories about major league baseball players. Andy, a freelance journalist, was responsible for writing the stories. Andy conducted all of his business activities via a close corporation called Baseball Stories, Inc., of which he was the only employee. Ruth was responsible for maintaining TBA's computerized subscriber lists, mailing the newsletter every month, and billing TBA subscribers. Molly provided all equipment necessary for TBA. Andy, Ruth, and Molly expressly agreed to the following: Molly would have exclusive authority to buy all equipment necessary for TBA; and TBA's net profits, if any, would be equally divided among Andy, Ruth, and Molly.

Andy subsequently wrote a story in the newsletter stating that Sam, a major league baseball player, had been taking illegal performance-enhancing drugs. Andy knew that the story was not true, but wrote it because he disliked Sam. As a result of the story, Sam's major league contract was terminated. While writing the story, Andy's computer failed. He bought a new one for TBA for $300 from The Computer Store. The Computer Store sent a bill to Molly, but she refused to pay it.

Sam has sued Andy, Ruth, Molly, TBA, and Baseball Stories, Inc. for libel.

The Computer Store has sued Andy, Ruth, Molly, and TBA for breach of contract.

1. How is Sam's suit likely to fare? Discuss.

2. How is The Computer Store's suit likely to fare? Discuss.

QUESTION 5: SELECTED ANSWER A

1. Sam's Suit

1-1. Does Sam have a valid claim for libel against Andy?

The issue is whether Sam has a valid claim for libel for the story Andy wrote. In order to claim a libel, a plaintiff must show that (i) there was a defamatory statement, (ii) of or concerning the plaintiff, (iii) which was published, and (iv) resulted in a harm to the plaintiff's reputation. When the plaintiff is a public official or a public figure, the plaintiff must also show (i) the defendant acted with malice, and (ii) the defendant's statement was false.

Defamatory Statement of or concerning the Plaintiff. For a claim for a libel, the defamatory statement cannot be a mere name calling but in general must allege a specific fact that is harmful to the reputation of the plaintiff. Also, it must identify the plaintiff. Here Andy wrote a story in the newsletter stating that Sam, a major league baseball player, had been taking illegal performance-enhancing drugs. The article specifically identified Sam and it specifically alleged that Sam took illegal performance-enhancing drugs. Therefore, there were allegations of specific acts of wrongdoing that were allegedly committed by Sam. Therefore, Andy's article constitutes a defamatory statement of or concerning the plaintiff.

Publication. Publication requires that the defendant share a defamatory statement at least with one person other than the plaintiff. Here Andy published his article in the newsletter with subscribers. Therefore, there was clearly a publication.

Damages. In a libel case, damages to the reputation can be presumed if the plaintiff meets all the requirements for defamation and also show malice and falsity. A libel is a publication of a defamatory statement in a written form. Here, as will be discussed below, Sam should be able to meet all the requirements so the damages can be assumed. Also, the article constitutes a libel as it is a publication in a written form with subscribers. Even if the damages were not presumed, Sam's major league contract was terminated as a result of Andy's story. Thus, Sam would be able to show he suffered harm to his reputation as shown by his losing the contract. Therefore, Sam can show damages.

Malice. Given the constitutional protection of free speech, a public official or a public figure must meet a higher burden of proof in order to win in a defamation suit. A public official is a government official and a public figure is a figure well known in the society, such as celebrities or professional sportsmen. A public official or a public figure must show, in addition to the 4 requirements of defamation that the defendant acted with malice. In this context, in order to show malice, a plaintiff must show that (i) a defendant had actual knowledge that his statement was false, or (ii) a defendant acted with reckless disregard to the truth of his statement. Here Sam is not a public official but he is a public figure. He is a major league baseball player, not just a local player who plays for a hobby. Thus, Sam must be well known in the society and is a public figure. Thus, he must show that Andy acted with malice when he published his story. Andy published his story knowing that it is false because he disliked Sam. While the fact that he acted out of personal grudge or dislike of Sam does not show that Andy acted with malice, the fact that Andy published a defamatory article about Sam knowing that it was false shows that he acted with malice for purposes of defamation. Thus, if Sam can prove that Andy knew that the story was not true, Sam would be able to show Andy acted with malice.

Falsity. A public official or a public figure must also show that the defendant's story is not true. Here the facts indicate that Andy's story was not true so Sam should be able to meet this burden.

In conclusion, Sam is likely to succeed on his claim on defamation against Andy.

1-2. Is Baseball Stories, Inc. liable to Sam?

The next issue is whether Baseball Stories, Inc. ("BSI") can be held liable for Andy's libel. Andy, a freelance journalist, conducts all of his business activities via a close corporation BSI, of which he was the only employee. Under the theory of respondeat superior, an employer is liable for the employee's tort if the employee committed the tort within the scope of his employment. While an employer is not generally liable for an employee's intentional tort, the employer could still be liable if (i) the employee was motivated by a desire to further the employer's interest, (ii) the tort was authorized or ratified by the employer, or (iii) the tort was part of the nature of the employee's job.

Here Andy and BSI's businesses consist of writing articles for journals. Thus, Andy's publication of the article in the newsletter was within the scope of his employment. Here Andy is likely to be liable for intentional tort because he was not merely negligent in publishing the story but he intentionally published the story knowing that it was false. Sam can argue that Andy was motivated by his desire to increase subscription and popularity of the newsletter and BSI's business of publishing articles. Thus, Sam can argue that BSI should be held liable for the defamation committed by Andy.

1-3. Can Andy be held liable to Sam, notwithstanding Baseball Stories, Inc.?

A person is always liable for his or her own tort. Thus, Andy should be directly liable for the libel against Sam. Also, a court may pierce the veil and hold a shareholder liable for the tort committed by the corporation if, for example, (i) the shareholder did not treat the corporation as a separate entity and did not observe corporate formalities, or (ii) the corporation was inadequately capitalized. This is most likely in a closely held corporation and even more so when a plaintiff is a tort victim who did not rely on the limited liability of the corporation. Here BSI is a close corporation and Andy is the only employee. Thus, it indicates that Andy had a controlling influence over BSI. While a corporation can have a sole shareholder and only one employee, the corporate formalities must be observed in order to maintain the limited liability status of the shareholder. Thus, if Andy commingled his personal funds with BSI's, used BSI's funds as if they were his own, used BSI's other assets as his own, or he inadequately capitalized BSI, Sam may be able to show that Andy and BSI are alter egos and Sam may be able to pierce the veil to reach Andy's personal assets for tort liabilities. Having said that, Andy should be directly liable to Sam in any case because it was tort committed by him personally.

1-4. Did Andy, Ruth and Molly form a partnership when they launched TBA?

Given that Andy and BSI can be held liable for Andy's libel, the next issue is whether Ruth, Molly and TBA can be held liable for Andy's libel. A partnership is formed when two or more people agree to carry on a business as co-owners for profit. No specific formalities are required to form a general partnership and whether the parties intended to form a partnership does not matter as long as there was an agreement to carry on a business enterprise for profit. Here Andy, Ruth and Molly decided to launch a business called The Batting Average (TBA). It is not clear from the name what type of entity they intended to form. However, it was formed to publish a monthly newsletter with stories about major league baseball players. Also, there is no indication it was intended to be a non-profit organization. In fact, Ruth was responsible for maintaining the subscriber lists and billing the subscribers. Also, they expressly agreed that TBA's net profits, if any, would be equally divided among Andy, Ruth and Molly. Thus, they agreed to form a business venture of publishing articles about major league baseball players for profit. Also, an agreement to share net profits shows that they formed a partnership. It does not matter that they never used the word "partnership" or they never intended to form a partnership.

The next question is what type of partnership Andy, Ruth and Molly formed as a result to determine their and TBA's liability. A default partnership is a general partnership where all partners are liable for their liabilities of the partnership. A creditor of the partnership must first look to the assets of the partnership and if they are insufficient, they can pursue the partners' personal assets. Therefore, in a general partnership, the partners act as guarantors for the partnership liabilities. There are other forms of partnership or business enterprise that provide some form of limited liability for some or all owners, such as a limited partnership, limited liability company, a limited liability partnership or a corporation. However, they all require filing a form of certification with the Secretary of State and they each require that their names indicate a limited liability by including the words such as "limited partnership," "LP", "limited liability company", "LLC" or "Inc." or "Incorporated." There is no indication here that Andy, Ruth and Molly or TBA filed any certificate of limited partnership to form a limited partnership or a certificate of qualification to form a limited liability company, nor did they file articles of incorporation to form a corporation. Also, the name, "The Batting Average" does not have any of the words indicating that they formed a business entity with limited liability. Since no formalities were observed, they would also not be able to argue that they formed a de jure corporation. Therefore, Andy Ruth and Molly formed a generally partnership when they decided to launch their business TBA.

1-5. Can TBA be held liable to Sam for Andy's tort?

Given that TBA is a general partnership, the next issue is whether it or Ruth and Molly can be held liable for Andy's tort. A partnership is liable for tort committed by a partner in the scope of his partnership. Here Andy committed a tort while he was publishing the article for the newsletter published by TBA. Thus, TBA would be liable for the tort and Sam would be able to look to the assets of TBA. In a general partnership, all the partners are liable for the partnership liabilities if the partnership assets are insufficient to meet those liabilities. Thus, if TBA's assets are not sufficient to meet Sam's claim, Ruth and Molly could also be held liable and may be required to pay out of their own personal assets. However, Ruth and Molly may be entitled to indemnification from Andy since Andy was the tortfeasor.

In conclusion, Sam is likely to be successful on his libel claim against Andy. In such event, (i) TBA and BSI would likely be vicariously liable and (ii) if the assets of TBA are insufficient, Ruth and Molly would also likely be liable out of their personal assets.

2. The Computer Store's Suit

The issue is whether (i) Andy, Ruth and Molly formed a partnership, (ii) Andy had an express, implied or apparent authority when he bought a computer for TBA, (iii) TBA can be held liable for Andy's contract liabilities, and (iv) Ruth and Molly can be held liable.

2-1. Did Andy, Ruth and Molly form a partnership?

As discussed above, Andy, Ruth and Molly agreed to carry on a business venture of publishing monthly newsletters for profit and to share any net profits derived therefrom. They did not make any necessary filings with the secretary of state and TBA does not have a name indicating limited liability. Therefore, TBA is a general partnership.

2-2. Did Andy have an Express, Implied or Apparent Authority when he bought a computer for TBA?

The next issue is whether Andy had an express, implied or apparent authority when he bought a new computer for TBA for $300 from The Computer Store. All the partners of a partnership are considered agents of the partnership and they are generally authorized to act on behalf of the partnership relating to the partnership's business, although each partner's authority may be limited by agreement. Under the agency theory, a principal can be held liable under the contract entered into by the agent if the agent had an authority to enter into such contract. An authority can be actual or apparent. An actual authority arises when the principal either expressly grants the authority to the agent either by words or conduct or it is implied from (i) the past course of dealing between the principal and the agent, (ii) the principal's past acquiescence, or (iii) such authority is incidental to other express authority granted to the agent.

Here Andy is a partner of TBA and thus he generally had the ability to act on behalf of TBA. However, Andy, Ruth and Molly expressly agreed that Molly would have exclusive authority to buy all equipment necessary for TBA. Therefore, Molly had the exclusive and express authority to buy all the equipment, including a computer used in the business. Since her authority was exclusive, Andy did not have an express authority to buy computers on behalf of TBA. There is no indication that TBA or Molly acquiesced in the past in Andy buying a computer. The Computer Store may argue that Andy was responsible for writing articles for TBA and thus using and buying a computer was incidental to his authority to write articles for TBA. However, given that buying equipment was Molly's exclusive authority, it is unlikely that Andy had any authority to buy equipment or computers on behalf of TBA.

The next question is whether Andy had an apparent authority to buy computers. An apparent authority arises when the principal holds the agent out to a third party as having certain authorities or powers. Given that TBA is an enterprise with only three owners and Andy was one of them and given that Andy was writing articles on behalf of TBA, The Computer Store is likely to argue that Andy had an apparent authority to buy a computer. On the other hand, TBA can argue that the fact that The Computer Store sent a bill to Molly indicates that they were aware that Molly was responsible for purchasing equipment. Also, the fact that Andy wrote articles for TBA can also only mean that he is an employee of TBA or a freelance writer. Thus, TBA may have a viable argument that Andy had neither actual nor apparent authority when he bought the computer and thus it should not be liable under the contract. However, even when the agent did not act with actual or apparent authority, the principal can be held liable if the principal later ratified the contract, which can be either express or implied if the principal kept the benefits of the bargain. Here, if TBA kept the computer and used it, there is likely to be ratification and thus TBA would be liable for $300 to The Computer Store.

2-3. Can Andy, Ruth and Molly be held liable for breach of contract?

Assuming that Andy acted within the scope of authority on behalf of TBA when he bought the computer or TBA later ratified the contract by keeping the benefits, the next issue is whether TBA's partners, Andy, Ruth and Molly can be held personally liable. As discussed above, they formed a general partnership. In a general partnership, partners are liable for the partnership liabilities. Thus, if TBA's assets are not sufficient to meet the liabilities to The Computer Store, they can each be held liable and required to pay out of their personal assets.

QUESTION 5: SELECTED ANSWER B

General partnership

A general partnership is an association between two or more people to carry on as co-owners a business for profit. There are no formalities required to form a partnership. There is no writing requirement or filing requirement with the Secretary of State. The subjective intent of the parties is immaterial. All that is required is that they intend to carry on as co-owners a business for profit. In other words, a partnership is formed, simply by meeting the definition of a partnership. Here, Andy, Ruth and Molly decided to launch The Batting Average (TBA), a business to publish monthly newsletters with stories about major league baseball players, and agreed to assign responsibilities among themselves for the management of the business. Furthermore, the sharing of gross profits gives rise to a presumption of partnership formation. Here, Andy, Ruth, and Molly expressly agreed to share TBA's net profits equally among themselves.

Andy, Ruth, and Molly formed a general partnership.

Sam v. Andy

General partners are always liable for their own torts. Thus, if Andy is found liable for libel, he will be personally liable for the tort regardless of the liability of TBA.

Libel

A prima face case for libel requires a defamatory statement, of or concerning the plaintiff, publication, and damages. In addition, when the defamatory statement concerns a public figure, such as a major league baseball player, the plaintiff must prove falsity and fault. For the fault requirement, a public figure must prove actual malice. Actual malice exists when the defendant knew that statement was false or recklessly disregarded the truth or falsity of the statement. Here, Andy wrote a newsletter stating that Sam, a major league baseball player, had taken illegal performance-enhancing drugs.

Defamatory statement of or concerning the plaintiff

A statement is defamatory if it adversely reflects on the plaintiff's reputation. Here, the statement that Sam was taking illegal performance-enhancing drugs clearly lowers his reputation in the community and in his profession. In fact, his major league contract was terminated due to Andy's newsletter. Furthermore, while the facts do not present the newsletter, it is safe to assume that Andy at least mentioned Sam by name. As a result of the newsletter, Sam was terminated.

Publication

For publication, the defamatory statement must be made to a third person who understands it. This requirement is clearly satisfied as Andy published the story in a newspaper.

Damages

Sam suffered general and special damages. For libel, damage to reputation may be presumed and as his contract was terminated, Sam has also suffered pecuniary loss.

Falsity and Fault

The facts state that Andy "knew that the story was not true". This would satisfy both additional requirements for constitutional damages as the statement is in fact false and Andy acted with actual malice when he published the newsletter knowing it was not true. The fact that he wrote the story because he disliked Sam would not establish actual malice, but his intentional disregard for the truthfulness of his statement satisfies.

Thus, Sam will be successful in a suit against Andy for libel.

Liability of Baseball Stories

In terms on Baseball Stories' and TBA's liability for Andy's tort, the issue is whether Andy was acting as an agent and whether he was acting within the scope of his employment and/partnership. An employer/partnership will be vicariously liable for torts committed by agents/employees/partners that are within the scope of scope of employment/partnership. Sam would argue that because Andy conducts all of his business via Baseball Stories and is its only employee he was acting within the scope of his employment and Baseball Stories is vicariously liable.

Liability of TBA

A partnership is vicariously liable for torts committed by agents of the partnership that are within the scope of the partnership. General partners are agents of the partnership. Thus, Andy is an agent of TBA and TBA will be liable for Andy's tort if he was acting within the scope of TBA.

Sam could also argue that Andy was working on a computer purchased for TBA, and Andy was responsible for writing stories for TBA; thus he was acting as an agent of TBA and within the scope of his partnership.

Liability of Molly and Ruth

General partnerships are jointly and severally liable for all partnership obligations. Thus, a tort judgment creditor may sue any general partner for his entire loss. However, the creditor must first exhaust partnership resources before seeking payment for partners individually. Thus, Sam could hold Molly and Ruth personally liable for Andy's tort, but Sam must first exhaust TBA's resources. If he fails to do so, Molly and Ruth could look to the partnership for indemnification and/or contribution from the partners.

2. Computer Store's suit

A partnership will be liable for contracts entered into on its behalf by agents who have actual or apparent authority or contracts that have been ratified by the partnership. Partners are agents of the partnership. Thus, Andy, Ruth, and Molly are agents of TBA.

To determine whether the principal (TBA) will be bound if must first be determined whether the agent (Andy) had actual or apparent authority or the TBA ratified Andy's purchase.

Actual express authority

There is actual express authority when such authority is granted in the four corners of the partnership agreement or expressly granted by a requisite vote. Here, Andy, Ruth, and Molly agreed that Molly would have exclusive authority to buy all equipment necessary for TBA. There were no changes made to this agreement by the partners and Andy did not receive permission from Ruth and Molly to purchase a new computer for TBA. Thus, Andy did not have actual express authority.

Actual implied authority

There is actual implied authority, when the agent reasonably believes he has authority based on the manifestations of the principal. As stated above there have been no such manifestations by TBA. Furthermore, it is unreasonable for Andy to believe he has such authority because the partnership agreement between him and Ruth and Molly expressly grants such authority to Molly.

Apparent authority

Apparent authority is based on the reasonable expectations of a third party. Where a principal holds out an agent as possessing authority and a third party reasonably relies on such holding out, there is apparent authority. While TBA has not made direct representations to The Computer Store on behalf of Andy's authority, generally partners have authority to enter into contracts in the ordinary course of partnership business. Furthermore, apparent authority may be created by an agent's title. For example, if Andy told The Computer Store he was a partner of TBA, such an expression would reasonably induce The Computer Store to rely on Andy's authority as a partner. Thus, even though Andy did not have actual authority to purchase the computer for TBA he likely had apparent authority, which would bind TBA for the contract.

Ratification

Ratification occurs where an "agent" purports to act on behalf of the principal when in fact he does not have actual or apparent authority, and the principal subsequently ratifies the action (with full knowledge of its terms). There are no facts to suggest that TBA ratified Andy's purchase and thus ratification is not available to bind TBA.

Liability

As mentioned above, general partners are personally liable for partnership obligations. Thus, if apparent authority is found, The Computer Store will have a claim against TBA, Andy, Ruth, and Molly.

Even though Molly will be personally liable to Computer Store, she may seek indemnification from TBA and may also seek contribution from Andy and Ruth as partners. In addition, Ruth and Molly and likely to have a claim against Andy for violation of the partnership agreement.

QUESTION 6

In 2011, Tess, age 85, executed a valid will, leaving all her property in trust for her grandchildren, Greg and Susie. Income from the trust was to be distributed to the grandchild or grandchildren then living each year. At the death of the last grandchild, any remaining assets were to go to Zoo for the care of its elephants.

In 2012, the court appointed Greg as conservator for Tess, because of Tess's failing mental abilities.

In 2013, the court authorized Greg to make a new will for Tess. Greg made a new will for Tess leaving Tess's entire estate to Susie and himself outright. Greg, without consulting Tess, then signed the will, in the presence of two disinterested witnesses, who also signed the will.

In 2014, Tess found a copy of the will drafted by Greg, and became furious. She immediately called her lawyer, described her assets in detail, and instructed him to draft a new will leaving her estate in trust to Susie alone and excluding Greg. Income from the trust was to be distributed to Susie each year. At Susie's death, any remaining assets were to go to Zoo for the care of its elephants. The new will was properly executed and witnessed.

In 2015, Tess died. That same year, Zoo's only remaining elephant died.

Zoo has petitioned the court to modify the trust to provide for the care of its animals generally.

1. Is Zoo's petition likely to be granted? Discuss.

2. What rights, if any, do Greg, Susie, and Zoo have in Tess's estate?
   Discuss. Answer according to California law.

QUESTION 6: SELECTED ANSWER A

1. Zoo's Petition to Modify the Trust

Trust Creation

The issue is whether Tess's will created a valid charitable trust. A trust may be created either inter vivos or by testamentary trust in a will. A trust is created when there is a present intent to create a trust, a trust beneficiary, a trustee, a trust res, and a valid trust purpose. Here, it appears that Tess intended to create a trust via her will and that her property was the trust res. Although Tess did not name a trustee, a court will ordinarily appoint an appropriate trustee rather than allow a trust to fail for lack of trustee. The trust has appropriate beneficiaries because the portion of the trust intended for the benefit of Tess' grandchildren has identifiable and ascertainable beneficiaries, and the valid trust purpose of supporting the grandchildren from the income.

A charitable trust is a trust for a public charitable purpose, such as health care, education, or religion. A charitable trust may be of perpetual duration and need not identify ascertainable beneficiaries. In addition, the doctrine of cy pres applies to charitable trusts. When a charitable purpose becomes impossible or impracticable, under the doctrine of cy pres the court will determine whether there is an alternative charitable purpose that comes as near as possible to the settlor's charitable intent or whether the settlor would prefer the trust to fail. Here, the remainder of the trust after the death of the grandchildren is a charitable trust because the assets are to go the Zoo for the care of the elephants. Because the elephants died after Tess's death, her express charitable purpose of caring for the elephants is no longer possible. However, it is likely that the court will apply cy pres to direct the trust to the Zoo for the care of other animals or to another zoo with elephants for their care. It is not clear that Tess had a specific connection to this Zoo or to elephants in particular during her lifetime, such that she intended the trust to remain valid only if Zoo took care of elephants with the money. Rather, it appears that she had a general charitable intent, and the court will direct the trust funds to the charitable purpose as near as possible to her intent. Accordingly, Zoo is likely to be able to modify the trust under the cy pres doctrine.

(The gift to the Zoo does not fail under the Rule Against Perpetuities because it vests in the Zoo within 21 years after a life in being at the time of the creation of the trust. Under the Rule Against Perpetuities a gift will fail if it need not vest within the time of a life in being plus 21 years. The grandchildren were lives in being and the trust passes to the Zoo immediately upon the death of the last grandchild. Therefore, the gift over to the Zoo does not violate RAP. The charity-to-charity exception does not apply because the grandchildren are not a charity.)

Conclusion

The court will likely grant Zoo's petition to modify the trust to provide for the care of its animals generally under the doctrine of cy pres.

2. Rights to Tess's Estate

Validity of 2013 Will

The issue is whether the 2013 will validly revoked Tess's 2011 will. Generally, a validly executed will may be revoked by an act of physical revocation or by the execution of a subsequent valid will that either expressly revokes the earlier will or is inconsistent with the terms of the earlier will. If it is inconsistent in terms, the earlier will is revoked only to the extent of the inconsistency. The later will must be validly executed with all of the required formalities. A will is validly executed when there is testamentary capacity, present testamentary intent, the will is in writing, the will is signed by the testator (or signed at her direction and in her presence), there are two witnesses who jointly witness the signature or affirmation of the signature, and the two witnesses sign the will before the death of the testator with knowledge that it is the will they are signing. If the witnessing formalities are not observed, it may nonetheless be considered a valid will if the will proponent provides clear and convincing evidence that the testator intended the document to be her will. Holographic wills are permitted in California if all material terms are in the testator's handwriting.

Here, Tess executed a valid will in 2011 pouring her property into a trust that was created by the terms of the will. In 2013, Greg attempted to revoke the earlier will by making a new will that was inconsistent with the earlier will by making an outright gift of all of the property. Thus, the 2011 will was properly revoked if the formalities were observed by the 2013 will. Because the court appointed Greg as conservator and authorized him to create a new will for Tess, Greg's capacity and present intent to create the will are at issue. No facts indicate that Greg did not have capacity or that he did not presently intend to create the will in 2013. The will was in writing and Greg signed it on behalf of Tess. Although Tess did not direct that he sign the will (and indeed she was not even aware of it), Greg had been appointed conservator and so he was authorized to sign on her behalf. The will was signed in the joint presence of two disinterested witnesses, and they also signed the will before Tess's death. Thus, all of the formalities were observed and the 2013 will became Tess' valid will, revoking the 2011 will by implication.

Undue Influence or Abuse of Relationship

The issue is whether the will or some portion of it was invalid because Greg exerted undue influence or abused his conservatorship in some way. Undue influence occurs when a person exerts influence over a testator to the extent that the testator's free will is overcome. If that happens, the portion of the will that was made because of the undue influence is invalidated. If that portion was made to a person who would take by intestacy, the gift is invalidated only to the extent of the intestate share. Undue influence is presumed where a person is in a confidential relationship with the testator, had a role in procuring the will, and an unnatural gift results. Here, Greg has not exerted undue influence over Tess because he did not need to prevail on her to change her will. Instead, he was appointed conservator and given authority to change the will himself. Thus, the gift will not be invalidated because of undue influence.

However, the court might decide that Greg abused his position as conservator by changing the will in a way that was contrary to Tess's intent, without ever consulting her as to her wishes. A conservator generally has fiduciary-like duties to the individual he is representing, and thus he must act loyally and in her best interests. Greg's change of the will benefitted him directly, in a way directly contrary to Tess's express wishes at a time when she had mental capacity. Thus, the court might find that Greg's conduct violated his duty to loyally represent Tess's interests. In that case, his gift would likely be reduced to his intestate share. However, if Tess's property passed by intestacy, it would go equally to Susie and Greg as Tess's only living heirs. This is exactly the will that Greg made. Therefore, Greg would receive the gift he gave himself when he was abusing his authority. In that case, the court might impose a constructive trust on Greg's property for the benefit of Zoo.

(In practical effect, Greg's wrongdoing does not matter because Tess was able to execute a valid will revoking his 2013 will, see below.)

2014 Will

The issue is whether Tess's 2014 will properly revoked the 2013 will created by Greg. As stated above, a will is created when there is present testamentary intent, testamentary capacity, a will in writing, signed by the testator, witnessed by two joint witnesses, and signed by the witnesses before the testator's death.

Testamentary capacity exists when the testator understands the nature and extent of her property and knows the natural objects of her bounty. Here, when Tess called her lawyer in 2014 she was able to describe her assets in detail and provide a reasonable explanation for leaving her assets entirely to Susie. Although Greg will argue that she lacked capacity because he had been appointed conservator in light of Tess's failing mental abilities, testamentary capacity may exist even when the testator lacks capacity to manage his finances and other personal affairs. Under the circumstances, it appears that Tess had capacity to understand her assets and who she wanted to leave them to, and the court will likely find that she had capacity.

Tess also appeared to have present testamentary intent because she instructed her attorney to draft a new will. The facts also state that the will was properly executed and witnessed. Therefore, the 2014 will validly revoked the 2013 will because it was completely inconsistent with that will.

Accordingly, at Tess's death in 2015, the 2014 will leaving her entire estate in trust with income distributed to Susie during her lifetime and remaining assets to the Zoo at the time of Susie's death was Tess's valid will.

Omitted Child

Greg might attempt to argue that he is entitled to an intestate share of Tess's estate as an omitted child. If a child born after the creation of a will (or the testator mistakenly believed the child was dead or did not know he had been born) is unintentionally omitted from the will, the child may take his intestate share and all other gifts are abated. However, Greg is a grandchild not a child, and he was alive at the time the will was made and intentionally omitted because Tess was angry that he had attempted to change her will. Thus, Greg will not be entitled to an intestate share as an omitted child.

Remainder to Zoo

As noted above, the gift to Zoo after Susie's death does not violate the Rule

Against Perpetuities. It is a valid charitable trust, and the court will likely apply cy pres to prevent the trust from failing.

Conclusion

Greg has no rights in Tess's estate. Susie has a right to income from the trust during her lifetime and Zoo has a right to distribution of the trust assets upon Susie's death.

QUESTION 6: SELECTED ANSWER B

1. Zoo's Petition.

The Issue here is whether Tess created a valid will and trust that left Zoo any interest in T's property.

2011 - Will

A valid will must be in writing. It must be signed by the testator in the presence of two disinterested witnesses at the same time who also sign the will.

The facts state that T created a valid will, so we can assume she met all elements of the will. Therefore, a valid will was created.

Trust

T left all of her property in trust for her grandchildren. In order for a trust to be valid, there must be a testator, a beneficiary, trustee, trust purpose, and trust property.

Testator

Here, T is the testator.

Beneficiaries

T's grandchildren Greg and Susie are the income beneficiaries b/c they get the income from the trust. The Zoo is also a beneficiary and they hold a future interest in the property. The Zoo will get the remainder of the trust after the last grandchild dies.

Trustee

Although there isn't a named trustee, it doesn't defeat the trust. The court will appoint a trustee if there is no trustee to manage the trust.

Trust Purpose

The purpose of the trust is to provide income to the grandchildren for their lives, then the remainder goes to the zoo.

Trust property

T has left all of her property into the trust.

Therefore, a valid trust was created. Under the 2011 will, Zoo had an interest in T's trust.

2013 - New Will

The issue is whether the new will is valid b/c it was created by a court appointed conservator.

Will Formalities

See rules above.

Here, Greg as the conservator for T and under the court's authorization created a new will for Tess. The will was signed by two disinterested witnesses. However, T did not sign the will. But Greg will argue that as the conservator, he was permitted to sign on her behalf. So, technically, a will was properly created. However, I will discuss below why the will should be void.

Greg as Conservator

A court can appoint a guardian or conservator to act on behalf of a person who lacks the mental capacity to act on their behalf. They have the authority to make legal decisions, such as drafting a new will. However, a conservator still owes the testator a fiduciary duty of care and loyalty. The conservator must act in the best interest of the testator and not make any decisions that are self-serving and are directly adverse to T's interest.

Here, Greg was appointed as a conservator for T b/c of her "failing mental abilities." Although he is authorized to create a new will for T, he must uphold his fiduciary duties. Greg violated his fiduciary duties when he created T's new will without first talking to her about the will and determining whether she was okay with changing the will so that it left the entire estate to Greg and Susie. Instead, Greg disregarded her previous will and left the entire estate himself and his sister Susie, cutting the Zoo completely out of the will. The act of leaving everything to himself and his sister shows self-dealing and he has violated his duty of loyalty. Even though he was legally permitted to create a new will for Tess, he violated his fiduciary duty to T. Any attempt Greg makes to argue that he was within his right to draft the new will will fail b/c he violated his fiduciary duties. T's estate could sue Greg for violating this duties and seek a request to void the 2013 will.

Undue Influence

Additionally, the Zoo and T's estate will argue undue influence per se b/c there was a fiduciary relationship with the person who wrote the will and there was an unnatural devise.

Here, Greg is the conservator and in a fiduciary relationship with T. The devise was also unnatural b/c the original will never intended to leave the entire estate to Susie and Greg. Therefore, the Zoo and T's estate should be successful in voiding the will under undue influence per se.

DRR

Alternatively, the Zoo and T's estate could attempt to revive the original will under DRR.

Under DRR, a previous will can be revived if a most recent will was created under fraud or misrepresentation. Meaning that the testator created the new will because they were misinformed about something (i.e., a beneficiary had died when they were really alive). If that is the case, then the new will can be voided and the old will can be revived.

Here, T's estate and the Zoo will argue that T would have never created the new will that Greg created. Greg fraudulently misrepresented T's wishes for her will and created an unnatural devise. As discussed above, T never intended to leave her entire estate to Greg and Susie. There is nothing in the facts that suggests she had changed her mind since 2011. Therefore, the 2013 will should be voided and the 2011 will should be revived.

2014 Will Drafted by Lawyer

After T discovered that Greg created the 2013 will, T created a new will. The issue here is whether a valid will was created for lack of capacity.

Will Formalities

See rule above. Here, the facts state that the new will was properly executed and witnessed. So, let's assume that will formalities have been met.

Lack of Capacity

Generally, a person lacks capacity if they are unable to understand the nature of their estate, the nature of their relationship with family and friends, and the nature of their act of creating the will.

Here, the biggest problem is that the court appointed a conservator for T b/c of her failing mental abilities. Other than that, we don't know much about her capacity to create a will. We don't know if "failing mental abilities" equates to lack of capacity. Let's look at the elements for capacity.

Nature of the act

This element means that the T must understand the nature of her acts and conduct of creating the will.

Here, T appears to understand the nature of her act of creating the will because she saw the will that Greg drafted and became furious and contacted her lawyer to draft a new will. It appears that T understood the nature of her act b/c she knew that Greg's 2013 will was not what she intended and she knew that she needed to call her lawyer to draft a new will. Therefore, this element is met.

Nature of the estate

This elements means that the testator must understand the extent of and identify his property.

Here, T understand the nature of her estate and property b/c she revised her will describing her assets in detail and left her entire estate to Susie. Thus, this element is likely met.

Nature of relationships with family and friends

This element means that the testator must understand their relationship with family and friends - the people they are leaving their assets to.

Here, T seems to understand the nature of her relationships b/c she was so angry at Greg for what he did that she specifically excluded him from her new will. She left all of estate in trust to Susie with the remainder to the Zoo. Thus, this element is likely met.

Therefore, since T appears to have met all the elements for capacity at the time that she created the will, the 2014 will is probably the valid enforceable will. The 2014 will revokes all prior wills automatically. If the court agrees that T had capacity at the time that she created her will, then T's 2014 will is probably valid and Zoo has an interest in T's estate.

Cy Pres

The next issue is Zoo's ability to use the assets b/c the trust assets were left for the care of its elephants but they have no elephants. Under the Cy Pres doctrine, the court can modify a charitable trust purpose if the trust purpose has been frustrated.

Here, T's trust left anything remaining in the trust to Zoo for the care of its elephants. The facts don't indicate that Susie has died yet, so the Zoo's interest is still a future one. Because the Zoo doesn't have any present interest in the trust, the Zoo will most likely fail in petitioning the court to modify the trust purpose. Although the Zoo doesn't have any elephants at this time, they might have elephants when Susie dies. If at the time that Susie dies, the Zoo doesn't have elephants, then the Zoo might have a better chance at succeeding in modifying the trust purpose. If they are successful in modifying the trust purpose, the new purpose must also be charitable and the court will probably want them to keep the charitable purpose as close as possible to what the original trustor intended the purpose to be. Therefore, Zoo's petition is premature. The court should dismiss it at this time b/c they do not have any present interest and the purpose of the trust is not currently frustrated.

2. Rights of Greg, Susie, and Zoo.

See discussion above regarding the beneficiaries' rights.

Disposition

Greg

Based on the 2014 will, Greg has no interest in T's assets. Of course, if the court determines that T lacked capacity to create the 2014 will, then Greg might be able to income from the trust from the 2011 will. The 2011 will will only be valid, if the 2013 will that Greg fraudulently created is void and the 2011 will is revived.

<u>Susie</u>

Susie has interest in the trust income for her life under the 2014 will. As discussed above, the 2013 will is likely invalid, so Susie won't get share T's entire estate with Greg. If the court determines that the 2014 will is invalid, then Susie gets trust income for life under the 2011 will.

<u>Zoo</u>

Zoo has a future interest in the remainder of the trust for the care of its elephants under the 2014 will.